THE DIARY

Escape from the Black March

Arthur L. Lindsay

iUniverse, Inc.
New York   Bloomington

THE DIARY
Escape from the Black March

Copyright © 2010 Arthur L. Lindsay

iUniverse books may be ordered through booksellers or by contacting:

iUniverse
1663 Liberty Drive
Bloomington, IN 47403
www.iuniverse.com
1-800-Authors (1-800-288-4677)

ISBN: 978-1-4502-6533-1 (pbk)
ISBN: 978-1-4502-6534-8 (cloth)
ISBN: 978-1-4502-6535-5 (ebk)

Printed in the United States of America

iUniverse rev. date: 10/22/2010

Contents

Prologue

This is the true story of an Indiana farm boy James B. Lindsay. It began simply enough, but amazing twists of fate turned his life into an account worth telling. In his youth he was the leader among six brothers - even though Lawrence was five years older. Because he had such a bold confidence in everything he did, his younger brothers thought of him as their hero. He was tall, handsome, and intelligent – and none of them ever doubted he could do anything to which he set his mind. That same attitude was held also of neighbor boys who came to visit – especially the two Plate brothers from town, who were always quick to fall in line behind him. Yet he was never pushy. Instead he had a clever and inventive spirit, which made life interesting for those who followed – even to the excitement of raiding Ole Man Hershey's watermelon patch late at night. He also had the admiration of his three older sisters. And it seemed that even his mother had a special distinction for him. Of her eleven children (two had died in infancy) she never used a nickname for any of them – except "Jim".

It proved to be a hardscrabble existence for the George B. Lindsay family during the Great Depression in the 1930s. Being a sharecropper, George found it to be a daunting task trying to feed and clothe such a large family - to the point sometimes of seeming impossible. Finally, after years of trying to scratch out a living, he gave up on farming. In desperation he moved his family to the city in the summer of 1940, searching for work in what was still a broken economy. With six boys at home (the sisters had all married) they settled for a few months in a small, three bedroom, house in the north end of Kokomo – in north central Indiana. Jim and his brothers shared the two upstairs bedrooms – three boys in each bed. The house had no running water, though there was a hand pump in the kitchen. For convenience, an "out-house" was attached at the back door. The only heat was from a potbellied stove in the living room. Saturday night baths were in a washtub – the first one in had the cleanest water. It was from those humble circumstances that Jim's incredible journey began.

The Decade of the 1940s began to show relief from the effects of the Great Depression Even so, the Lindsays, along with many other families in America, were still struggling to make ends meet. Far worse, however, at the same time, evil rumblings were beginning to disturb the world. The dogs of war were barking - howling. Daily there were ominous reports of the expanding war in Europe on the part of the belligerent Germans; who pushed ruthlessly against their neighbors. Meanwhile, on the other side of the globe, the Japanese continued a relentless, cruel, and devastating march throughout the Far East. This bombardment of military news aroused an excitement in young Jim Lindsay. He was certain that war for the United States was on the way and he wanted to get into the action. That was not just a heroic ambition on his part - he was eager and serious about it. But he had a major problem: he wasn't old enough. Having just turned 17 in June of 1941, he was ten months shy of the military's minimum age required for enlistment.

Jim, however, was so determined that this was what he wanted to do – had to do – that he came up with a solution: he would lie about his age. But in order to do that, he needed for his mom and dad to agree not to contest his enlistment. When he told his parents of his plan, his mother especially was adamant – she did not want him to go. "I'm not going to lie about your age," she declared. "You have just one year left in high school. Finish that, then you can go."

But Jim was not so easily dissuaded. He knew he had to be obedient to his parents, but he was nonetheless determined to accomplish his plan. So he resorted to the only way he could think of to change their minds - he went on a hunger strike. His younger brothers couldn't understand refusing to eat perfectly good food (more for them though) – especially with such an outstanding cook as their mother. Jim, however, was unwavering in his plan to skip his senior year of high school and join the fledgling Army Air Corps. It took only four days of his refusing to eat before his tenderhearted mother couldn't stand it any longer. His parents relented and he left for Indianapolis to begin his service record on September 5, 1941.

Sure enough, the following form letter arrived the next week, signed by 1ˢᵗ Lt. J. G. Kiplinger at the United States Army Recruiting Office at Fort Benjamin Harrison, Indiana. Oddly, it was not addressed to anyone in particular – the army too was anxious to get every recruit it could:

This letter is to advise you that James Benjamin Lindsay enlisted on Sept. 5ᵗʰ, 1941 in the Regular Army of the United States for Air Corps, Jefferson Barracks, Missouri for a period of three (3) years.

He gave his age as 18 years, 2 months, and stated that he is not married, and no one is dependent upon him for support. He named as his nearest relative Verda M. Lindsay (Mother), 700 North Bell St., Kokomo, Indiana, and as the person to be notified in case of emergency.

The form for written consent to his enlistment in the Regular Army bears the signature of none.

Should any of the statements made by the soldier, as indicated above, be incorrect or misleading, or if there is any other irregularity in connection with his application for enlistment of which you are aware, it would be proper for you to communicate this knowledge to his Commanding Officer. For this purpose there is enclosed an official envelope, which requires no postage, addressed to his first Commanding Officer.

This letter has been shown to the soldier in order that he may reaffirm the answers he gave, as indicated above, to question in connection with his application for enlistment.

True to her word, his mother did not lie for him. When the letter arrived she read it carefully, then merely tucked it away in a drawer in her dresser. Though she wanted him safe at home, she made no answer. His dad also kept mum on the matter. But - if the truth were known - he was secretly proud of his boy who bore his middle name - Benjamin. Yet the whole idea of military service was strange to both of his parents; neither knew anything about it (George was exempted from service in World War One because of the need for him to farm). For that matter, they were like everyone else in the country - few people in America had paid any attention to those in uniform since "Johnny came marching home again" in 1918. The United States had quickly demilitarized after The Great War and less than one percent of the population was in the

Army or Navy in 1941. From the entire Lindsay clan, Jim was the first to join – but he wouldn't be the last. It was becoming a dangerous world. Eventually he and his five brothers would serve a total of 47 years in various branches of the military.

His mother was uncertain and filled with concern when her son went away. But neither Jim nor his parents knew anything about the significance of the timing of his enlistment. Yet, even before he finished his basic training, the country would be thrust into a brutal and worldwide conflict. With the dastardly, unprovoked bombing of Pearl Harbor by the Japanese on December 7, 1941, the sleeping giant on the North American Continent was stirred into action. For twenty years, throughout the twenties and thirties, loud-voiced and self-indulgent isolationists had kept the United States out of world affairs. In spite of President Wilson's vehement urging, the Senate wanted nothing to do with the League of Nations and would not ratify the treaty. Having put forth a valiant and costly effort in bringing World War One to a powerful conclusion against the Germans, the prevailing attitude in the whole country was for peace and tranquility. That became an even more widely accepted sentiment as the withering effects of the Great Depression began to fade. As Franklin Roosevelt was overwhelmingly voted in for a second term in 1936, his campaign theme song "Happy Days are Here Again", became the mood of the country.

Not only that, but then Americans wholeheartedly bought into the attitude of British Prime Minister Neville Chamberlain and accepted his assurance of "peace for our time", after his dubious meeting with Adolph Hitler in Munich, Germany in 1938. Indeed, up to the time of those dark and sinister surprise attack moments against Honolulu on that Sunday morning, the United States had seemed secure. After all, two wide oceans separated "the land of the free and the home of the brave" from everyone else in the world. Why should Americans care if those strange foreigners were determined to kill one another?

Yet in a matter of cruel minutes on that bloody Sunday morning the world of peace was quickly shattered!

Jim Lindsay had been specific in his enlistment plan. He had his heart set on being a part of the Army Air Corps. Ever since, as a boy, he had seen his first airplane land at the small airfield across from his grandmother's farm on Highway 31, just south of Kokomo, he had wanted to fly. Now he was intent on belonging to the Air Corps even though it was not a separate part of the military – just a branch of the Army. The air superiority of the Japanese at Pearl Harbor proved to be certainly devastatingly efficient. Before that, however, the German Luftwaffe (Air Force) in its domination of Poland in 1939 and its four-day-conquest of the Low Countries in 1940 began to arouse the attention of the military brass in America. Having entered the First World War rather late, the United States didn't have much experience from those earlier aerial battles. For American pilots the tales of the "Red Barron" and the "Blue Max" were matters of legend – but it was celebrity for which they longed.

The major impediment to being well manned and well equipped was the fact that the Air Corps existed as a branch, subordinate to the United States Army - even until 1947. Up until the initial experiences of World War Two, air power was considered useful only in support of ground troops.

Nevertheless, change was on the way. By the time Jim became a part of the Army Air Corps in 1941, its ranks had swelled to 152,125 men and 6,777 aircraft – fighters and transports – but there were only a handful of bombers. Even so, that was an eightfold increase from the meager force that existed in 1936. That particular growth was in response to President Roosevelt's special message to Congress on January 12, 1936, in which he declared that because of the threat of impending war in the world, America's air defenses were woefully inadequate. Acting rather quickly for that legislative body, on April 3rd Congress allocated the $300 million FDR had requested for expansion of the Air Corps. At the start of that buildup the Air Corps had requested 50 B-17 Flying Fortresses, which had first come into production in July 1935. That particular request, however, was denied. Members of Congress, who considered themselves experts on such matters, declared that there were no strategic requirements for aircraft of such capabilities. Consequently, by 1938 there were only 13 on hand and orders for more had been scrapped.

That shortsightedness was inexcusable, but was speedily overcome with the advent of war. Destruction from the sky became the military's major "advancement" in warfare. Because of that the B-17 became a key strategic weapon. Air Corps personnel had touted its outstanding features since the first prototype was introduced. It was a potent, high-flying (35,600 feet), long-range bomber (2,000 miles), capable of unleashing great destruction, able to defend itself and return to its home base even despite any extensive battle damage it may have incurred. By 1945 American workers would produce 12,731 of the big beasts at a cost per unit of $238,329 (more than $3 billion 1940s dollars). During the air campaign against Germany, American aircraft dropped 1.5 million tons of bombs on Nazi installations. Nearly half of that total, 640,000 tons, came from the bays of B-17s – more than from any other airplane. Accuracy from as much as five miles up was outstanding because of the use of the then-secret Norden bombsight. They pounded German targets from the west by the Eighth Air Force departing from airfields in England - and from the south by the Fifteenth Air Force, flying from bases on the Italian Peninsula. By 1944 it was not unusual for those two commands to put as many as 3,000 bombers, along with their fighter escorts, in the air to destroy German installations.

The once mighty Luftwaffe could not withstand such an onslaught - even with its introduction into the conflict in 1944 of the first ever jet fighters. But that innovation came too late to make a significant difference on behalf of the Germans. At about that same time also came the most devastating blow to the air power of the Nazis in what was later heralded as "Big Week" – February 20-25, 1944. For five continuous days the Eighth Air Force, flying out of Great Britain hit steadily at German aircraft production facilities – destroying the possibility of replacement aircraft for the Luftwaffe. The demoralizing accuracy of that campaign forced the Germans to disperse aircraft manufacturing eastward to a safer part of the Reich. Ironically, it was because of this move eastward that in 1945 the encroaching forces of the Soviet Union gained access to the advanced German technology. The postwar result was a very rapid development of Soviet Air Force jets based on the captured German wartime technology.

James Lindsay was but one of more than half-a-million Air Force personnel who served in the European Theater. Early in 1942 he had begun training as a gunner for the B-17. The gigantic airplane had been dubbed a Flying Fortress because of its ability to defend itself against fighter aircraft of the enemy. There were thirteen powerful .50 caliber M2 Browning machineguns on board. There were four double-barreled turrets in the nose and tail, and in bubbles above and below; one at each waist position; two beside the cockpit; and one in the lower dorsal position. By the time he was assigned to Italy in November 1943 as a part of the newly formed 15th Air Force, Jim had proved himself proficient as a left waist gunner and had gained the rank of Technical Sergeant. The campaign against German targets became intense, and to keep pace crews were flying as many as six or seven missions a month. There would not have been much time for relaxation if it had not been for the periods when torrential rains poured on Italy, keeping the bombers grounded.

It was during one of those periods of forced relaxation that Jim experienced an episode that he wrote home about. Remarkably, that letter - written on November 10, 1944 - was to be the last letter his family received from him from Italy:

Dear Mother,

I received three letters from you. One was mailed September 26. I was glad to hear that you received four of the money orders OK.

There isn't much to write about, so I will tell you what I did last night. We have a laundry man now and he lives out behind our camp. He invited three of us over to his house for supper and told us how to get there. We left camp about five and started out across the fields. We walked and walked and then it started raining and we walked some more. We arrived at his home about seven and of course we were a little bit wet.

The old man brought out some wine and then brought out a little table and put it in front of us about the time we got set down. Then one of his boys came through the door with a rope. Well it was so funny that I laughed until I cried, because there was a mule on the end of the rope. We moved our table over and he led the mule through the bedroom and out into the kitchen.

The old man then brought in three plates of spaghetti and it tasted so bad that we could hardly eat any of it. We finally told him we had enough. So he said he would bring in the roast.

Well this is also a joke, but nevertheless I ate roast sparrows. They had them cooked heads and all. I pulled the head off of one of them and laid it aside, but the old man didn't want to see it go to waste. So he picked it up and ate it, saying "molto buono", meaning very good.

That was too much for me. So we left as soon as we could. What a night!!!

I have eight more letters to answer so I will cut this short. I hope you won't mind.

Loads of love,

Your son, Jim

Shortly after mailing that letter, early the next morning in fact, the weather cleared and Jim and his crew headed north for what was to have been his 45th and last mission. The Air Force had determined that was the maximum risk any airman should have to face. The B-17 in which they flew was noted for its ability to absorb battle damage, still reach its target, deliver a devastating payload, and bring its crew back safely. It was not built, however, to withstand the bizarre mid-air disaster with which this story begins.

Chapter One

AN INCREDIBLE 4½-MILE PLUMMET TO EARTH

Jim Lindsay and the right waist gunner – in fact all ten crew members on the aircraft - were relaxed in their seats after a successful bombing raid over Salzburg, Austria. They had flown back over the Alps and were due to land in less than an hour at their home base in southern Italy. Jim was elated – in the next few days he would pack his bags and head for the States.

But the euphoria of the moment was not to last.

Suddenly everyone on board was alerted to danger by cries of alarm from the rear of the plane. "Go down! Go down!" The tail gunner exclaimed, screeching at the top of his voice as he tried frantically to slide backward out of the most vulnerable position on the B-17 Flying Fortress. His anguished shouts reverberated throughout the full 74-foot length of the gigantic aircraft. It took only a moment for his words to register with the pilot, but by then it was too late. The gunner was already dead and the plane was doomed to immediate destruction. He had been the first to see another B-17, which had been a companion in the attack, flying out of control. It slammed downward on top of the hapless airman and his airplane. Beyond him, because of the terrific impact at 200 mph, the practically indestructible aircraft was instantly torn apart all the way to the mid-section. Without warning there was a sudden suction of turbulence that pulled at everything in the disabled plane: men and equipment were exploded out into the 7-degrees-below-zero air, 26,500 feet above northern Italy, not far from the Yugoslavian border.

In desperation, the left waist gunner, 20-year-old Technical Sergeant James B. Lindsay, instinctively grabbed for the parachute stored at his feet as he went flying from the broken airplane, driven by a gale-like force into the atmosphere. Then, as he began to fall like a rock, he struggled to keep hold of the parachute – his only source of security in a situation of total instability. He pulled it tightly across his chest even as the wind threatened to tear it from his grasp. The two intense weeks of training he'd had at jump school had not prepared him for such a moment – he knew he'd have to improvise if he was going to survive. He looked down across his body, trying anxiously to hook the chute to his harness, but his oxygen mask was in the way so he couldn't see to make the connections. Then, holding the chute firmly under his right arm, he reached up with his left hand, unhooked his mask and threw off his helmet – it was useless to him now anyway – he wasn't connected any longer to the plane's oxygen supply – and he had already plummeted far enough that it wasn't needed, he could breathe freely.

Incredibly, it had been only two weeks earlier when he had discussed just such a scenario with his airmen buddies in the squad room back at their airbase, near Foggia in southern Italy. He had contended that it would be possible for a man to put on a parachute while in a free fall. But no one agreed with him. In fact, all the others had laughed at him with scorn. To a man they were certain that such a thing could not be accomplished. "There are just too many unpredictable variables," one man argued, "which would be impossible for anyone to overcome."

Now, could he prove them wrong and his theory right? Suddenly his life depended on it! There was no time for panic - but also no time to waste. Falling at a rate of 60 mph he realized that he had maybe ten minutes left – at the most - in which to accomplish the impossible – to deploy the chute and save himself.

Somehow, though it wasn't easy, he managed to maintain his composure in those moments of impending disaster. Even for one so young he had gained invaluable leadership experience and confidence since joining the Army Air Corps. Yet it was difficult to accomplish even the slightest move with the wind pulling against him, sapping at his strength. He couldn't just stand firm and put on his parachute as he normally did. Nonetheless, struggling with all his remaining energy he got the left hook snapped on, then at last the right hook and snap. As he looked down, the ground was rushing toward him at blinding speed. From the corner of his eye he could see that the waters of the Gulf of Trieste were perilously close. He jerked strongly, anxiously at the ripcord and gulped a sigh of relief as – thankfully, amazingly – air began to flow into the chute. By then he was less than 1,000 feet above the ground. A strong, swirling wind was blowing from the north, threatening to collapse the chute. He pulled strenuously on the riser to steer away from the frigid waters. Having no survivor gear, he knew that landing in the frigid waters of the gulf could be disastrous.

Since the chute had not completely bellowed full of air, his descent was rapid, and he hit the ground with a thud. Fortunately, however, his landing was somewhat cushioned as he hit hard on the crest of a sand dune. The sand gave way under the sudden weight of his body. With no control of himself, he quickly slid about twenty feet down its western slope. He lay on his back for a long moment trying to figure out how, in the last ten minutes, he had accomplished the impossible. "What in the world?" He asked in amazement, realizing that at that moment he should be dead – but definitely he wasn't. Over and over he blinked his eyes as he tried to affirm in his own mind what had just happened, but it was beyond his understanding. What Providential hand had guided his descent? "Thank God," were the only words he could speak as he sat up - amazed. Other than a bit of stiffness from the landing, he was unhurt. He had avoided the icy waters of the gulf by less than twenty feet.

Slowly Jim pushed himself to his feet and looked at his watch. It was eleven o'clock in the morning, November 11, 1944. He didn't realize it at that moment, but oddly enough, it was exactly 26 years to the very hour that the Armistice to end World War One had been set. "The war to end all wars" had proved to be an erroneous, empty, and valueless declaration of politicians who thought of themselves as world leaders. Whatever plans some of them envisioned had not been very successful. Peace never did gain a foothold in Europe in the 1920s. Trouble and despair erupted continually in the minds of men – and women - because the victors had not been wise at all in their reparation demands on the losers – the Germans. Now, this enormous second war to destroy what had become an even greater and more deadly German menace was proving to be far more costly than the first. The ingenuity of man had created such powerful weapons of mass destruction that there were heavy losses both for the Allies and the Axis Powers.

If just considering the 15th Air Force, to which Lindsay was assigned, the cost/effectiveness was staggering. During its brief 18 months of operation from a complex of Italian airfields, it lost a total of 3,364 aircraft - and 21,761 airmen died in combat. On that 26th Anniversary of Armistice Day alone, the 15th lost a total of 44 aircraft – including one B-17 shot down over Salzburg, and the two in the tragic collision over Italy. There had been 220 bombers, along with their fighter escorts, in the air armada that day - to hit industrial targets at Rozenheim, Salzburg, Villach, Linz and Lienz; the railroad at Zell am Sea; the highway bridges at Sillian and Wurzen Pass; and railroad bridges at Pinzano. As the war had progressed, bombing raids against the German war machine were reaching deeper and deeper into enemy territory. The proud Fatherland of the "Master Race" had become a bountiful - almost daily - hunting ground for the relentless American and British bombers.

At the moment, of course, none of that was in the mind of Sergeant Lindsay. Instead his situation was critical, personal, and immediate. He was alone - on his own in a strange, unplanned circumstance. From his position at the bottom of the sand dune he had no idea of the lay of the land, exactly where he was, or who controlled that area. Italy had started the war in proud goosestep with Germany under the boastful leadership of dictator Benito Mussolini. But after devastating losses in North Africa and then in Sicily, as Allied forces began moving up the Italian peninsula, Mussolini was overthrown. Italy had surrendered to the Allies more than a year earlier on September 3, 1943. Then, three weeks after that, on October 13, the newly formed Italian government had declared war on Germany. But that did not end the matter. The Nazis resorted to being a vicious and brutal occupying army against its former ally. The *Wehrmact* (German Army) was determined to stand its ground. It had already lost the Africa campaign, which left Italy as the primary buffer for the Fatherland from the south. Consequently, a series of ruthless, bloody battles for control of the mountainous terrain had continued unabated.

Unbelievably, that struggle persisted on until May 2, 1945 – even after the German and Italian dictators were dead. That was four days after Mussolini was captured, executed, and hung upside down in the center of Milan. There the Fascist, who had claimed for himself the title "*El Duce*" (The Leader), had been scorned and his shirtless body beaten with boat oars by his own countrymen. It was two days after the German's own *Fuhrer*, Adolph Hitler, had committed suicide in a darkened, windowless bunker in Berlin. Incredibly, even with the loss of those leaders, the remnants of the German Army hung on, retreating back to that northern area of Italy. The lonely garrison in Venice was one of the last of the German forces in Europe to quit the fight and lay down its arms.

Of course Jim knew none of that. The end of this unbelievably brutal, globe-spanning war was still more than six months away.

For mid-November, the weather that day was unusually mild and there was not a sound of anyone around. As he listened, the only noise he heard was the gentle swishing of the waves on the nearby shoreline. The young airman had been so preoccupied in his own frantic effort to get to the ground safely that he hadn't looked around for other parachutes or seen where the wreckage of his plane had fallen. He could only assume that because of its speed, the shattered pieces would have gone into the gulf. But what about his captain and the co-pilot, or his other seven buddies? Was he the only survivor? He choked back a sense of loss. In the course of flying one mission after another in the war effort – along with the many days of companionship between flights - they had become close friends. "But now's not the time for sentiment," he declared in a whisper to himself. "I have to keep my wits about me. I'm on my own."

Digging furiously with his hands, Jim dug a hole in the sand and buried his parachute. In case the enemy was on the scene, they would have seen the crash and would be looking for survivors. He knew he had to be on the move – and he had no weapon with which to defend himself. Hurriedly he got beyond the shoreline and crawled along a dry ravine on his belly. From there, for more than three hours, he scurried from one hiding place to another, purposefully heading south – toward possible rescue and freedom. Fatigue was beginning to set in because he had been up since 3:00 a.m. To get to its target over Salzburg, Austria that day, Lindsay's plan had taken off at four o'clock in the morning.

Such timing was significant strategic planning by the Air Force. Though the B-17 was the workhorse of the 15th Air Force with its long-range ability to hit targets deep inside enemy territory - normally it was only used for daylight bombing, because then it was less vulnerable to German interceptors that would attack formations of the gigantic aircraft like swarming bees. But the gun crews of the Flying Fortress were powerfully effective in full daylight when they could see clearly. In fact, when flying in a tight deployment, they were fashioned into a practically impenetrable fortress in the sky - against which the highly acclaimed German *Messerschmitt* fighters had exasperating difficulty in their attempts to strafe the massive bombers. German pilots likened attacking a B-17 combat formation to encountering a *"fiegendes Stackelschwein"* – a flying porcupine.

It was late afternoon when Sergeant Lindsay finally came upon a lonely looking farmhouse in an open field. Not knowing where he was - but thinking that more than likely he was in German controlled territory - he decided to take a chance. He knew he couldn't get through enemy lines on his own - he had to trust someone. Jim, who was typically decisive, said in encouragement to himself, "Well, here goes." Since he had had good relations with Italians in the south of Italy near his airbase, he walked boldly toward the house. As soon as the first face appeared he said with a smile, *"Buon giorno."* ("Good day.")

Because of his flight uniform he was readily recognizable to the farmer and his wife, who greeted him excitedly. Though they didn't speak or understand English, he tried to explain with sign language and his limited knowledge of Italian that he was trying to evade capture. "Si, si, si," they assured him as they welcomed him into their home.

Like most houses in Italy, it was of stone construction, but with a high-pitched roof because of the frequent heavy winter snow in that region of the country. The main room of the house was large, but very sparsely furnished with three bunk beds stacked on each side. "I guess this is where the family does most of their living," he assumed to himself.

At the wife's invitation he sat down at a roughly hewn wooden table. She brought a plate of dry bread and cheese, and encouraged him, *"Mangia! Mangia!"* ("Eat! Eat!") He chewed at it thankfully and washed it down with a cup of water.

The farmer, who had been pacing nervously near the door, pointed to a lower bunk bed and indicated by his hands cupped against his cheeks that his guest should rest. Jim looked at his watch. It was straight-up 4:00 o'clock in the afternoon. With confidence in the kindness of his hosts, he agreed that a nap would be nice. He found it snug and warm under the woolen coverlet, and totally exhausted, he quickly fell asleep.

He did not hear when the farmer and his wife slipped out the door.

The scene was about to change – and not for the better.

About an hour later two young sons of the farmer, carrying vintage hunting rifles, came noisily into the room and shook him awake. They didn't point their weapons at him, but said calmly, "*Vieni con noi.*" (Come with us.). Being shocked out of a deep sleep, Jim wasn't certain what to do. His sense of trust was beginning to fade. But he couldn't confront two armed men – and the language barrier kept him from asking any helpful questions about their intentions. "Why didn't I take advantage of those language classes at the base?" He muttered angrily with a shrug of his shoulders.

Since their parents had been so kind, he could only hope that the sons were partisans and would help him through enemy lines and back to the American side. Outside they led him down to a small stream and indicated he should get into a boat that was tethered there. The older of the two men stood in the back of the boat, rowing gondolier style, while the other sat facing Jim – holding even more tightly to his hunter's rifle. They seemed amiable enough, but they ignored him and kept up a constant chatter with each other. At first he tried to decipher what they were saying, but since they were speaking in a local Venetian dialect, he didn't understand anything of their conversation. With obvious excitement they started upstream as the sun was waning in the west.

With time to think, the sergeant felt a deep sense of dejection due to the day's turn of events. He thought to himself, "How could this be happening on my final bombing mission?" In spite of the babble of the two brothers and the rhythmic sound coming from the slapping of the oar in the water Jim felt himself adrift in the loneness of the moment. "Hey, I have to stay alert," he challenged himself. "This is no time to wallow in regrets – I'll still be home soon."

So Jim cast aside any negative thoughts and to keep his mind active began to reflect instead on recent raids his crew had made. In August alone his bomber had hit the enemy hard on six different days. On the 3rd of August his squadron pounded industry in the Friedrichshafan area, including chemical and fabric works, and two aircraft factories. His plane was part of an armada of 600 B-17s and B-24s that slashed at the slender lifeline for the flow of materiel that ran through the Brenner Pass to supply German armies in Italy – bridges and viaducts were blasted. They also hit a torpedo factory, and rail and oil installations in Southern France; and once again hit rail and harbor installations at Genoa on the west coast.

Just three days later, with super effort on the part of the ground crews, the 15th put nearly 700 heavy bombers in the air over Southeastern France. Sergeant Lindsay's plane dropped its load of 4800 pounds of bombs on the railroad yards at Valence, and on the oil storage dump and railroad bridges at Le Pouzin, 15 miles to the south. Recalling that mission, a slight smile eased across Jim's slender face. "I didn't need to fire my machine gun even once," he recalled quietly to himself. "Only a few enemy fighter aircraft tried to respond to the attack."

August 10th took his flight eastward over Romania. More than 450 bombers joined together to hit six oil refineries in the Ploesti areas. The Eighth Air Force, flying out of England, had been pounding Ploesti for months, but the Fifteenth had first hit that target on April 5th. Through that combined effort from England and Italy, by the war's end - because of the relentless pounding from the air strikes - production of petroleum products at those facilities was down to a mere trickle of about 10% of their pre-war capacity.

Sergeant Lindsay considered the mission he flew on August 16th to be one of the most significant – as it was in support of troops on the ground, entering France. A total of 108 B-17s were used against bridges vital to German defenses. Jim's plane concentrated on St. Pierre d'Alibigny. Others hit two bridges across the Rhone between Lyon and Marseille.

Though details of the atrocities that the Germans were inflicting on Jewish men, women and children prisoners in Auschwitz was only beginning to eke out to the western world, Sergeant Lindsay was pleased to be in the air over that site on August 20. The targets for more than

460 B-24s and B-17s that day were three large oil production plants in Poland and Slovakia. While in flight he had yelled across to the right waist gunner, "Isn't this about where one of those big concentration camps is located?"

"Yeh, I think so," his buddy agreed.

"Then I hope the prisoners down there will be encouraged by the sound of the explosions coming so near to them," Jim declared.

"Or maybe they can even see the flames and smoke billowing into the air," his companion shouted back in agreement.

The final August mission for Lindsay's 95th Bombardment Unit was on August 23rd, when a total of 472 heavy bombers hit industrial plants in and around Vienna, Austria.

In spite of the uncertainty of his situation at the moment, a sense of satisfaction seeped into his thoughts as he reflected on those flights over the enemy. They had been both significant and inspiring. He realized that because of such efforts by him and others, the end was drawing near for the murderous intentions of Hitler's Germany. Now, with a lift of pride to his spirit, he recalled how often he had had a sense of thrill as he looked out of his bubble on the side of the plane and saw a tight formation of hundreds of American aircraft, flying with one mission in mind – to destroy the Hun. Now, however, he only wanted to get back to his unit – and then on home. But his reflections came to a quick end.

With his back to the front of the boat, Jim was only aware that they were reaching their destination as the boat began to slow. The young man in front of him lifted his gun slightly as a sly smile slipped across his face. The sergeant interpreted the look as sinister, and realized too late that he had put his trust in the wrong people. The rower, peering straight ahead, steadied his oar in the water.

Chapter Two
SOLD INTO THE HANDS OF SINNERS

Just minutes before the boat slowed to its destination Jim had checked his watch; it was now after six. During nearly two hours of the trip upstream the scenery had been quite boring - the area was bleak and deserted. With the onset of winter there was no sign of life anywhere – only the majestic Mediterranean Pine trees maintained a verdant green. Though the younger farmer kept a watchful eye on him, neither of the two Italians had addressed a word to him. Yet they spoke constantly, animatedly, to one another. Unable to understand their Venetian dialect, he had paid no attention to them. But when the rower announced excitedly in clear Italian, "*Guarda*!" (Look!) Jim's worst suspicions began to unfold before him. As he peered over his right shoulder the first thing he saw through the haze of the hastening dusk was a rickety wooden landing. Then, to his instant shock, he saw that the rocky shoreline was crowded with a platoon of German soldiers. They had been looking for him – or any other survivors - ever since they had witnessed the spectacular midair collision of the two gigantic bombers that morning. His first inclination was to dive into the water and try to swim away. But the young farmer, now revealing his true intentions, pointed his gun directly at the airman's chest. With a wave of the muzzle he indicated that Jim should climb out of the boat as it glided to a stop. With no apparent option, he silently complied.

Shouting at him harshly in German, two soldiers rushed forward to grip him firmly as he stepped onto the landing. With a curt expression of "*Dank*" ("Thanks") a third soldier leaned over to the boat and handed the rower some crumpled up Reich Marks. So much for trust – he had been sold for a pittance into the hands of masters who put little value on human life.

Immediately a sergeant came up to take control of the situation and began to aggressively search the American for weapons. He had none. But in the process the surly German stripped him of all his personal possessions – a watch, billfold with family pictures and money, and his dog tags. Then with a smirk on his face, looking directly into the blue eyes of the young American, with a harsh grunt of "*Dank*" in his voice, he twisted a gold ring off the prisoner's finger.

The Germans earlier had seized another American airman - the lieutenant co-pilot of the other airplane. These were the only two survivors from the two ten-man American crews. The Germans were laughing boisterously among themselves and insulting the prisoners with curses. In ridiculous fashion – though they had done nothing - they claimed success in having destroyed two enemy airplanes without firing a shot. In rough fashion they shoved the two airmen into a nearby barn without offering any food or water.

It was some relief to Jim to have a companion, though they had never met before since they were from different bomber command groups. Both of them were grieving over the loss of their crewmembers, because it was obvious that there were no other survivors. Then, speaking to one another in hushed tones so as not to be overheard by the Germans – and possibly divulge any vital information - the two of them shared their experiences of the morning.

"That's incredible!" The co-pilot declared when Jim had finished telling him of his practically impossible, yet successful fall from the sky. "That didn't just happen," he exulted. "There was Someone watching out for you."

"I know that for sure," Jim agreed. He then went on to tell of his hours of elusiveness and of the brief experience with the farmer and his wife and their two sons. "I thought I had to trust someone," he concluded, "but I sure made a dumb mistake."

"Ungrateful Italians," the lieutenant commented with a snarl in his voice in response to the story of betrayal. "But don't blame yourself.

You'd think that the way the war is going they'd not do anything to help the Germans."

"Money," Jim explained in one word.

"Yeh," the lieutenant agreed with a nod of his head, "greed is an overwhelming influence – especially in the worst of times."

He then began to explain what had happened that morning from his perspective. "Our plane was heavily damaged by flack in the raid over Salzburg," he began. "Fortunately for the rest of us, the bombardier had released his load of bombs just before an antiaircraft round exploded in the belly of our plane. The blast killed him instantly and he plummeted to the ground. But it also destroyed our rudder control cables. Our pilot, by maintaining a high altitude, did an incredible job of getting us back over the Alps. Without the rudder connection, however, we were at the mercy of gravity. We were flying blind, just hoping to be able to hobble back to base – 'on a wing and a prayer', so to speak.

"We didn't realize we were descending on top of your plane until the minute before impact. But before the captain had time to warn the rest of the crew, I knew there was no way we were going to be able to avoid the crash and I instinctively unbuckled my safety harness. Fortunately I had kept my parachute on - and when our two planes hit I was thrown through the canopy high into the sky – that's when I got this gash across my cheek. The Germans tracked my parachute as I descended and they captured me almost immediately. No one else from my plane made it out."

"That's a terrible conclusion to what had been a successful raid," Jim responded. "But it's evident that Someone was with you too."

"You are so right," the lieutenant agreed. "And as you guessed, the wreckage of both of our bombers fell piece by piece into the gulf. No one else made it out. There was nothing to do to help any of the guys who might have survived the crash."

"I wish I had some water to wash out that wound," Jim said sadly. "It doesn't look good."

"I'll live," the lieutenant replied sardonically.

It was well after midnight - in the early hours of the next morning when they were each taken individually into the farmhouse for questioning. Though he was certain that he had no significant information to share, Sergeant Lindsay – in spite of threats - repeatedly only gave his name, rank, and service serial number. He kept to himself the reflections he had had earlier of successful bombing raids.

Exasperated at not being able to gain any information, finally the Germans shoved both men back into the barn.

Though he was dead tired, Jim could not really sleep. Drifting in and out of consciousness, he kept reliving the mid-air collision of the two gigantic bombers and his unbelievable descent. The slightest recollection still took his breath away. "Surely," he thought, "God had a hand in it." Again and again he reflected on the preaching of Pastor Ruby at the small evangelical church he had attended in north Kokomo. "God has a plan for you, Jim," Ruby had assured the young teenager repeatedly whenever they met privately. "Don't ever forget Romans 8:28:

And we know that in all things God works for the good of those who love him, who have been called according to his purpose."

Thankfully, he remembered.

But in spite of his certainty that there had been Sovereign intervention on his behalf that morning, he questioned himself harshly as to being so dumb to be captured without a fight. "Could I have avoided the Germans and Italians altogether and somehow have gotten back to our lines?"

Then, after only a few hours of fitful sleep on the barn floor, yelling guards awakened the two prisoners. *"Rasch! Rasch! Mit du!"* ("Quick! Quick! With you!") A soldier insisted to Jim as he poked him with the muzzle of his rifle. Though his knowledge of German was limited – but soon to be expanded – the message to hurry was clear. Jim got to his feet as quickly as he could. At gunpoint the two prisoners, with a guard and driver, were squeezed into a tiny three-wheeled motorized contrivance (these were quite popular in fuel-starved Italy). For two hours they headed northward, bouncing over rough roads - finally pulling to a stop at a huge chalet (a Swiss-style mountain home). Without a word of explanation, the two of them were confined to a small, roofless, walled-in courtyard - then more waiting and uncertainty. The mountain air was blowing down from the Alps. They huddled together as it grew increasingly cold. At last they were offered the first food of their incarceration - a sandwich of dry bread with a salami-type of meat in it. Even that seemed like an afterthought. There was no apparent plan on the part of the Germans of how to care for prisoners – just be sure to hold onto them.

Next, though they were visibly shivering, the two airmen were put into an open, horse-drawn wagon. They bounced along a rugged road several miles to an airbase. There they were shoved into a barracks that was outfitted with beds, but there were no blankets. Just after he had nodded to sleep - about an hour later - the door of a side room opened. A sergeant pointed at Jim and, and with a wave of his hand, ordered him in, leaving the lieutenant companion behind. A German captain, seated behind a table, began an intense interrogation as the prisoner – backed by two guards – stood across from him. The short, squat captain tried to humiliate the now weary prisoner, laughing at how easy it had been to capture him. "Like a <u>dummkopf</u> (idiot – literally, dumb head) you walked right into the home of our good friends and then took a nap!

"No wonder you're losing the war," he snarled.

("Oh, yeh! Haven't you been paying attention to the news?" Jim questioned to himself.)

On the table the captain had laid out the sergeant's few possessions that had been taken from him at the time of his capture. He read aloud the information on the dog tag. "This is you – *ja?*" He asked harshly.

"Yes, sir," Jim responded without comment.

"Where are you based in Italy?" The German asked in a soft suggestive voice.

The American airman only stared at him.

"What was your target today?" The captain asked with a tinge of anger in his expression.

No response.

"Don't you know I could have you shot, if you refuse to answer me?" The officer demanded.

"Not according to the Geneva Convention," the American answered softly.

The captain eyed him coldly, calculating how he might break down his will and secure more information. To raise the prisoner's anger, the captain fitted Jim's ring on his own finger and held it up to the light to admire it. (Jim treasured that ring. His mother had sent it to him for his 20th birthday.) "I like the black onyx setting," the German said with a lilt in his voice. "I must say it is quite beautiful." Then he made a show of snapping the prisoner's watch on his own wrist. He rifled through the billfold and stuffed the money in his pants pocket. He pulled out a picture. "Your mother?" He asked.

No answer.

The captain tore the picture in two and threw it in a wastebasket.

Though enraged on the inside because of the insult to his mother, Jim didn't even break a frown or smile.

Quietly the German read a news clipping stuffed in the billfold. "Hmm, interesting," he said as he laid it aside. Throughout an hour of standing there, Sergeant Lindsay continued – no matter what question the officer asked - only to repeat his name, rank, and serial number. He never saw his possessions again.

Finally he was ushered back into the bunkroom and the co-pilot was taken in for questioning. The lieutenant's session lasted only about thirty minutes. Then the two of them were allowed to get a few hours of sleep. In conferring with one another they were both satisfied that they had given no information useful to the enemy.

Early the next morning they were awakened and provided with a slice of dry bread and a cup of coffee.

Pointing to the open wound on the lieutenant's cheek, Sergeant Lindsay asked the server, "Can you take care of this man's injury?"

"No time," a nearby German sergeant replied. At once they were marched off to a railroad yard, where a train heading north was belching out steam as it waited for them to arrive. With guards shouting their hurry-up orders in German and threatening them with the butts of their rifles, they were herded into a tiny compartment on the train. It was already crammed with six other airmen prisoners. Instantly, as the door was shut behind them, the train lurched forward – with a series of clanking noises as each car in succession was pulled into line. The six who had been confined there already for more than a day were quick to explain that there were no amenities available – and by common consent they had designated one corner in which to relieve themselves.

Whenever the train screeched to a halt in small towns along the way, German soldiers would open the door to ask about the effectiveness of their anti-aircraft flak – anxious to be able to brag to their superiors. But the questions were never lengthy, nor did they stay long. The stench was becoming unbearable – and anyway, the Americans never gave them a positive response.

When night came, Sergeant Lindsay climbed up on the compartment's coat rack to try to sleep. It was only twelve inches wide, but he decided that it was better than hunkering down on his haunches on the floor like the others. Even so, he could not rest. In his mind he kept condemning himself continually for trusting the Italians. "I will never make that mistake again," he affirmed to himself. Still, there was no sleeping for him or any of the others – just a dazed listlessness.

The next morning guards opened the door to provide breakfast for the prisoners – one loaf of bread for the eight of them and a pot of chicory –diluted coffee, but only two mugs. This proved to be their only food for the day. They yearned for something to eat, but there was nothing. Their stomachs growled in distress. Early the next morning - it was the same meager offering – dry bread and questionable coffee. They traveled, starving like this, for two more days. The train squealed to a stop at every little station along the way. The resulting hunger pangs made it difficult to concentrate on anything but to worry about food. "Do these Germans intend to starve us into submission?" One of the men asked angrily. But there was no apparent answer, just growling empty stomachs.

On the fifth day the train started through the Brenner Pass, which is nearly 4500 feet above sea level. The snow was deep and the weather was cold – and the prisoners had only one means of heat - that was to huddle together – taking turns at being on the fringe.

When two of the airmen realized where they were, they began laughing. One said to the other, "Remember when you had this railroad yard in your sights during our bombing run in August? We tore this place apart."

"Yeh," his friend laughed, "it was the most effective sortie we ever had – every bomb was on target."

"Me too," Jim chuckled, "my bombardier dumped his whole load on this place in that first week of August."

But their laughter was short lived as they were all thrown into one another, two of them tumbling to the floor. The huge steel wheels screeched against the tracks as the train slammed to a sudden stop. Their bombing had indeed proved successful – the tracks ahead had been reduced to a spaghetti-like tangle of steel – twisted and torn.

The Germans didn't take long in opening the compartment door and ordering the eight airmen outside and into the snow. Though it was bitterly cold, at least they could breath deeply in the fresh air. Fortunately, the guards allowed them to stomp around to try to keep warm as they waited - for what they knew not – there had been no further instructions. As they lingered there, they marveled at the view ahead – what they had helped to destroy. It was surreal. There was not a living thing in sight. Bits of cement railroad ties hung high in midair, suspended on steel rails, which had been blasted upward. "What destruction!" the lieutenant exulted. "It reminds me of what a forest looks like after being ripped apart by a tornado."

"Yeh," an airman agreed, "just bare kindling left over."

The devastation stretched beyond their view.

As the prisoners shivered in the snow, it took about an hour for the Germans to bring up a rickety old bus – a vintage World War One leftover. They began ordering the prisoners onto it. Regular passengers on the train, seeing what they considered preferential treatment for the Americans, jumped down out of the train to attack the prisoners. But the guards, acting in strict military fashion, cordoned off the entrance to the bus, shielding the Americans from the shouting civilians.

The bus ride, however, was not lengthy – only about two miles to get beyond the bombed out section of tracks. There they were fed a watery potato soup along with hunks of black bread before being herded like cattle into a boxcar of another train. Though there were already other prisoners there, they at least had room to lie down. Later that night – no one knew what time it was, only that it was very dark and dreary – the train started a speedy transit of Austria. "Very crafty of the Germans to make this run at night," the lieutenant said to the rest of the prisoners. "This way they avoid the possibility of being bombed out in the daylight."

A communal sigh of resignation crept over the prisoners as they lay down to sleep. They received no comfort from hearing the rhythmic rumbling hum of the wheels against the tracks below them. They knew instead that mile-by-mile they were being carried deeper and deeper into the heartland of Germany – far, far from family and the possibility of rescue. "What are they up to?" Jim questioned to his companions. "It's obvious that the Germans have no master plan – just a 'hurry up' to take us north."

From a darkened corner came an ominous reply, "They may seem bumbling and disorganized, but the sinister thinking of these Nazis means that they have a special plan for us … each of us … all of us."

Early the next morning the train slowed to a stop. With the engine still belching smoke the boxcar door slid open and they were ordered by the now familiar shouts of, "*Rasch! Rasch!*" to jump down onto the frozen ground. From a nearby tent, two men dressed as kitchen helpers, carried a pot of hot soup between them and set it on a table. They then ladled out bowls of the watery substance – with a hint of a potato in it – and handed one to each man. "At least it's hot," Jim mumbled to the man next to him. No sooner had they finished their "breakfast" than he and the other seven prisoners from Italy were singled out and marched a quarter-of-a-mile to a side street. A military truck, a green-slatted Opel Blitz (Lightning) 3000, which was the most popular vehicle used by the German army, was waiting for them. Obviously it had experienced the effects of war. Its protective canvas cover for the top had been ripped to shreds. The eight of them climbed aboard, accompanied by the two guards that had been with them since their first train ride in Italy. With a cold wind blowing down on them, they had a clear view of the countryside. It seemed that just about every other building had been turned to rubble from the incessant bombing runs of the allies. "Hey, look," one of the GIs said pointing to a huge sign. "At least we know where we are – Frankfurt."

Knowing it was nearing the end of his responsibility with these prisoners, one of the guards yelled to the driver, "*Halt!*" The truck pulled to a stop in front of a *Gasthaus* (Inn) just inside the city. The driver and one guard went inside and came out with two big pitchers of beer and a stein for each man. "You have been good prisoners," the older guard said in perfect English – the first he had spoken in their six days together – as he poured out beer for each man.

Such an incongruity on the part of his captors fascinated Jim Lindsay. "You never know," he said to the airmen to his right, "what to expect out of these guys next." Nonetheless, though the beer was warm, it was a tasty treat and each man savored it to the last drop.

But that was the end of the party - there was to be no more Mr. Nice Guy. The truck drove on and into a civilian prison. There they were ordered to remove their boots or shoes before being locked all together in one cell. It proved to be a long, uncomfortable night as the eight of them took turns using the three narrow bunks that were built against the walls. Though this seemed to be unbearable, it was the last thing that even resembled kindness that Sergeant Lindsay was to experience at the hands of Germans. Things were to become excruciatingly worse. The next morning the Americans were taken to a military prison, which was constructed of open-slatted wooden barracks through which the winter wind blew at will. The lieutenant was separated from the noncoms and led away without a chance for farewells. His cheek was swollen bright red and scabbed over. Jim never saw him again.

There was no exercise yard for this prison – men slept, ate, and sat wearily inside the buildings day after day.

But Lindsay soon didn't even have that. On the second day - without any explanation - he was moved into solitary confinement. It was a small, windowless room in the basement. There were no amenities in his stonewalled room – just cold cement. To relieve himself he had to ask a guard to take him to a toilet – which was only a latrine. There was no commode, just a big hole in the tile floor. With no water in his segregation cell, there was no way he could bathe himself. Having always been very meticulous in his appearance, he resorted to sucking his fingers to clean them. (Though not very effective, it was a process he would have to put into practice many times in the future – and never with satisfactory results.)

Besides the loneliness of the isolation, he suffered the uncertainty of why he was being singled out for such harsh and underserved treatment. What had he done that they should be so angry with him – to set him aside without food or water? What sinister plan did they have for him? Though he couldn't understand what they were saying, he knew that their whispers were about him. Along with the growing pangs of hunger, those mounting doubts also kept him from any restful slumber.

Chapter Three
A SPY – REALLY?

Being a Prisoner of War of the Germans was bad enough in itself, but to be singled out for unwarranted harsh treatment was more than Sergeant Lindsay could comprehend. Nor could he understand why he was then subjected to a nightmare of intense interrogation. It was evident from their attitude and their determined procedure that the Germans were convinced that they had a firm case of espionage against the young American, but they gave him no hint of their purpose. Every day, for five straight days he was taken before a German officer and interrogated for six or eight hours – being taken back to his cell in the middle of the day for about an hour. (Obviously the officer needed a break.)

The routine became unbearably boring – it even gnawed at his brain in the hours he had to himself. Each morning he was given a single slice of bread – three times there was a little bit of jam on it. There was nothing more to eat during the day until he was given a bowl of questionable soup in the evening. In effect, he was not provided a morsel of anything substantial to alleviate his hunger pangs. This lack of any sustaining food proved to be a stress on his whole system. He thought constantly of food – wondering, for instance, what his mother might be fixing for dinner that night – almost able to taste it, but denied the satisfaction of even a tidbit.

After the first two days of questioning, Sergeant Lindsay wondered to himself, "I suppose this guy is one of their experts, but how can he maintain his sanity, asking the same stupid questions over and over. What's he up to? None of this makes any sense." But on the third day fear raised its ugly head for a moment when the interrogator declared, "We know you are a spy! We have proof!"

Jim made no response, but only looked at him dumbfounded. He had no idea what the German was thinking or talking about. What sort of "proof" could they possibly have for such an accusation?

"You were in the Asian Pacific Theater before you were sent here. What was your assignment there?" The interrogator insisted, waving a scrap of paper back-and-forth in his clenched fist.

At least Jim now knew why he was being given so much attention. The very absurdity of the matter almost caused him to chuckle out loud, but he smothered the impulse with coughing. True, he had been part of a unit assigned to the Pacific Coast of the United States for nine days – June 2-11, 1942. In his wallet he had carried a notice that he had received the Pacific Theater Ribbon, but he had cut out the date and place of issue. The first captain who had interrogated him in Italy – and stolen all of his possessions – had passed on that bit of information. Grasping at straws, the Germans tried to make something significant of it.

Sergeant Lindsay decided to stay mum, and took pleasure in his supposed part in espionage purposefully - he said nothing to refute the charge. "Let them waste their time on this for as long as they want," he reasoned. "At least they'll not be focusing on anything important."

"Why are you here?" the German insisted again and again, certain that he could uncover a clever plot on the part of the young American and his superiors. But his questioning was totally inconsistent - his process incompetent. Instead of focusing on the prisoner and truly interrogating him, he would talk endlessly about just anything and everything that mattered to him. Often he muttered along in German – and Jim had no idea of what he was saying. He would rant and rave about the wide destruction of his homeland by the prisoner and his fellow "criminals" of the American Air Force. Then often, even in mid-sentence of talking about something else, he would turn to preaching about the master race – even bringing himself to tears whenever he invoked the name of his beloved *Fuhrer*, Adolph Hitler.

In order to endure the boredom of such sessions, Lindsay amused himself by picturing the direct opposite of what the interrogator was boasting about. "According to him," Jim reasoned to himself, "the description of the icon of the master race is a tall, handsome, blond man with a strong athletic build. But where's his model? Look at him! This guy is only about 5' 6", with straggly black hair, and crooked teeth – and ugly ole Hitler certainly doesn't match up either."

Each session began with the officer sitting behind a desk. Then the prisoner was marched in to sit across from him seated on a three-legged stool. Sometimes, as the German got carried away in his emotions, he exchanged places with the prisoner. In all the five days – a stunning thirty hours - of worthless interrogation, Lindsay never said a word - except to repeat his name, rank, and serial number. He began to think that the monotony would never end. Yet unknown to him, the German was even more frustrated than he was. The captain finally realized that his superiors had evidently been grasping at straws, seeking to uncover some great new strategy of the enemy, and hopefully change the course of the war that was going so badly for them. But their suspicions had been without merit, proved to be fruitless, and they finally gave up on the bogus matter.

At the end of a week, without explanation, Lindsay was taken alone to a different, much smaller prison in Frankfurt. He never again saw the other prisoners who had been with him on the arduous trip from Italy. At the front desk of the prison, a slender-faced corporal ordered, "Take off your flying boots and set them on the counter." Without a word Jim complied. In exchange he was given a pair of hard-soled shoes and a tattered sweater. The clever clerk smiled at how easy it was to intimidate the American. Greedily he then shoved the highly prized boots under the counter as his own possession.

During his one night there, in another dungeon-like atmosphere, he learned from others that he wouldn't be there long. "This is only a gathering place," another sergeant explained. "From here they ship prisoners to a wide assortment of camps." Then as an afterthought he continued, "You'd think that with the war going so badly for them that they could find a better use of their resources."

Nonetheless, Jim realized that whatever the German scheme might be for him, the lifestyle would likely only go from bad to worse. Unfortunately he was right.

The next day, he was again singled out from the others and taken alone by car to a railroad yard, where he was locked into a boxcar with thirty other American airmen POWs – all non-commissioned officers like himself. The train was composed of five such prison-cars-on-wheels. It shortly chugged to life. The prisoners had no idea where they were headed, but it was evident to all that the Germans had a plan as the train headed eastward. The sinister purpose of that Nazi strategy was beginning to leak out to the Allied Forces. There were confirmed reports that the intent of the Germans was to use prisoners as human shields against advancing ground forces. This being contrary to any human standard of warfare, it drew widespread, angry condemnation in the American press. Since the Germans, under Hitler, had often proved that they were a law unto themselves, the threat was taken seriously.

Though concerned for his own welfare, Jim was even more disturbed when he saw many other boxcars – loaded with a cargo of men, women, and children – even infants - crammed together mercilessly. As they were being transported like cattle, anguished faces looked out from tiny, barred windows at the top of boxcar doors that were locked from the outside. "I wonder where they're headed?" He thought to himself. But if he had known the answer, his own spirit would have sunk even lower in dejection.

The stench of human excrement and urine in the boxcar became more and more offensive as the day progressed into days. The train of misery was shuttled to many sidings and connected to many different trains – and sometimes just sat in place for hours, but no one was allowed outside. It was not until the second day that the door was opened briefly. Two guards hoisted up a barrel of water with a ladle and a bag of two-dozen loaves of stale bread. Without comment, they quickly slammed the door shut and left the distribution of the meager supplies to the prisoners. The airmen didn't give their captors any satisfaction of fighting over it, Jim and another sergeant saw to it that everyone got at least a half-of-loaf of the bread.

The Germans had given them no instructions that they needed to ration that little bit of food. But the door never opened again with any offering of food or water. For five long days they hoped expectantly for more provisions – but there were none. With the passing of days a bread-and-water diet became excruciatingly clear to the prisoners. In fact, not knowing how cruel their captors could be, they had consumed that meager provision of bread on the first day. With each succeeding day they became increasingly weak and weary with thoughts of food gnawing at their empty stomachs as they bounced along in their stinking cage on wheels. Though they drank sparingly of the water, after four days even that was exhausted. The Germans had sound – though sinister reasoning in providing no further food to the prisoners; men weakened by hunger become more obedient and easier to control.

The prisoners did have one source of satisfaction, however, during the monotonous travel. As they rode wearily through one town after another they could peek through cracks in the wall to see the effects of their previous efforts - the bombed-out shells of buildings. Everywhere they looked there was widespread destruction. Then came a scary matter of minutes when the train passed through Berlin at the exact time the city was under a heavy bomb attack. The airmen knew that Flying Fortresses, at 35,000 feet, couldn't tell the contents of the boxcars – only that it was a German train and therefore a viable target. But no bombs fell close to them and they chugged on eastward without incident.

Late in the afternoon of the fifth day, the train pulled to a stop at its destination: Keivhide in Pomerania, Northern Poland. This region had always been considered by the Germans to be a key component of the Fatherland. At one time, before the First World War, this had been a proud part of Prussia, which was the central state in the formation of the German Empire in 1871. The Treaty of Versailles in 1919 had turned it back over to Polish control.

After standing still for an hour, the train door was slid open and the prisoners were greeted with bitter cold. The wind was blowing at gale force. The ground was frozen as solid as ice. Clothing on the prisoners was hopelessly inadequate; Jim had only the thin sweater given to him in Frankfurt and his flight jacket. The men had been shivering for the entire trip, but with some protection from the elements – now, out in the open there was none. The five boxcars disgorged more than a hundred and fifty filthy, weary, starving, dehydrated Americans. They had been without food for four full days. Guards, wrapped securely in heavy trench coats and carrying bayoneted rifles, marched the prisoners in a hurried fashion three kilometers to *Stalag Luft IV.* (The Germans divided their prisoners according to the captive's particular branch of service. The German word *stalag* was used to specify camps for Prisoners of War, and *luft* – air – was used to designate camps for Air Force personnel.) When they got to the camp, and were secured inside the barbed wire enclosed compound, these newly arrived prisoners were made to stand in a frigid formation until their name was called. Weakened by days without food, the men shivered in silence.

An hour later - totally numb with cold - when he heard his name announced, "Lindsay, James B.," Jim's first thought was of getting indoors to a source of heat. But that proved to be a false hope. Once inside he was told to strip naked, leaving his clothes in a pile on the floor. This was not a strip-search – to look for contraband. No, the purpose was to humiliate him. This was always a key, planned element of the Germans in controlling prisoners – to break their will to resist. For his part, Jim was determined not to shiver – not wanting to appear weak in front of his captors. The cold, however, had penetrated to his very bones and he shook noticeably. Without a word of explanation, a guard gripped his upper arm and shoved him into the next room to stand before the Camp Commandant, Lt. Col. Aribert Bombach. Humiliated and filthy, he was not thinking of anything militarily and failed to salute the man.

Infuriated, though much smaller than the prisoner, Bombach struck him first in the stomach, followed by a hammer blow on the right side of his face. Not expecting such treatment, and not on his guard, Jim was knocked clear across the room. As he struggled to his feet the officer demanded in perfect English, "Don't you know enough to salute a superior officer?"

In compliance, without a word, and with as much bearing as a naked man could muster, the American straightened to his full six feet and saluted the little 5' 6" German.

Smiling with a wry sense of satisfaction, Bombach returned to his desk, looked at a roster for the camp, and then ordered, "Put him in Lager C, barracks two, room two." All of that just to get a room assignment. But that was only the beginning; the sergeant would learn in coming months that every decision of the Commandant was designed to be as beastly to prisoners as possible.

With a guard standing over him, he redressed quickly and was taken to his assigned lodging.

Barracks two was of humble construction – like everything else in the sprawling compound – made of roughly sawed, unpainted wood. It had been thrown together hastily earlier that year, and received its first Americans on May 14, 1944. The four compounds (*lager* in German) were separated by double-fenced barbed wire. Each lager was designed to hold 1600 prisoners – a total of 6400. By the end of that year, however, it had become crowded with more than 9,000 American Air Corps noncoms. In addition to them there were 606 British, 147 Canadians, 37 Australians, 22 New Zealanders, 8 South Africans, 1 Norwegian, 2 French, 58 Polish, and 5 Czechoslovakian prisoners.

Bombach had total control over the lives of all these men in the camp, yet did nothing to care for the welfare of any of them. In fact, he was pleased with the overpopulating – it meant that much more misery for these prisoners whom he loathed. The commandant had a cadre of dedicated Nazis under him and he gave them free reign to be as brutal as they wanted. They, in turn, delighted in finding cruel ways in which to express what they supposed their superiority to be. Most notorious among them was Corporal Schmidt. He stood 6' 7" and was broad shouldered, but he was oafish and not well coordinated. In fact, he fit perfectly the name by which the prisoners dubbed him "Big Stoop". He was the triggerman for Sergeant Reinhard Fahrnert, who was in charge of security. Schmidt physically abused hundreds of prisoners and pilfered continually from their Red Cross supplies. He also delighted in intervening when prisoners attempted to swap the contents of Red Cross parcels with local civilians for eggs and other food. The price for being caught at such trading was instant death on both sides of the deal – and of course the items were confiscated.

Fortunately the prisoners learned to identify a few less-Nazified guards who could be bribed with cigarettes to round up small amounts of local food.

Stepping inside his new home away from home, Sergeant Lindsay was stunned by what he saw in the dim light of a single bulb hanging from the ceiling. Twenty-one men were crowded there already, sitting or lying on pallets of bedding on the floor – or leaning against the walls of the 20-by-20 square foot room. There were no beds for anyone. The so-called mattresses were nothing but wood shavings, stuffed inside coverings of heavy tan paper. Each man was allotted two blankets but no pillow. There was a pot-bellied stove in the middle but nothing else in the small room – not a single stick of furniture, any table or chair. Each man seemed to know which tiny spot on the floor was "his" and maintained personal property in a pile against the wall. The first sight for the newcomer was of an emaciated bunch of men – always on short rations – always scrounging for another scrap of food. In three weeks' time he himself had already dropped twenty pounds from his formerly robust and trim 180 – and during coming months of near-starvation he would lose much more.

Noticing the reddening raw scar on his right jaw, one of the men knowingly observed, "I see you've met our Commandant – he has a unique way of welcoming newcomers."

"You mean the little guy, with black hair slicked back?" Jim asked.

"Yeh," his new companion replied. "Among ourselves we call him Snaggletooth."

Several men snickered derisively in agreement.

"That fits him," Jim replied.

Three men in the farthest corner scrunched themselves together to make room for him on the only unused mattress on the floor. From around the crowded room the men proceeded to ask him all kinds of questions, anxious to hear any news from the outside world – some of them had been stuck there for six months already. But he had no current news to share. It was now December 4, 1944. He could only recount for them the incredibly long and painful three-and-a-half-week, thousand-mile trip from Northern Italy since his capture. But he told nothing of the air campaign he had experienced, because he suspected there might be a German stoolie in the mix of men. He had suffered the agony of the loss of his crewmates and had endured undeserved ugly treatment by his captors - which in coming months would only get worse. "But, I'm certain," he told them, "from all the destruction I've seen across Germany, that the war will be over soon and I'll be eating strawberry shortcake in Kokomo, Indiana, for my next birthday on June 18. No one makes shortcake like my mom – and she always has it fresh for me on my birthday – with whipped cream."

He spoke with confidence. He had set a goal. Though none of them could imagine such an outcome, they didn't laugh. They were certain that he too would soon get used to the fact that they were stuck in this particular "hell hole". They all had fallen into the funk of the boredom of their incarceration. At Stalag IV there was nothing to do but sit – and nothing good to eat. Those were two necessary resources of encouragement to the human spirit and they had neither of them. Yet no one argued with him – they were of the mind to let him have a bit of hope. Inwardly they doubted his prediction, but his words encouraged a few of them to dream for themselves.

Meanwhile, that same attitude of assurance was not being celebrated back home in Kokomo, Indiana. To the contrary, a dread of uncertainty prevailed in the home of his father and mother, George and Verda Lindsay – and with his brothers and sisters. His mother had complained many times from mid-November onward, "It's just not like Jim not to write." But she went ahead and sent his Christmas package to his post in Italy. Then the first note of distress came to them by Western Union telegram on November 26, just three days after Thanksgiving – but 15 days after the fact of his near-death experience:

The secretary of war desires me to express his deep regret that your son Technical Sergeant James B. Lindsay has been reported missing in action since eleven November over Italy. If further details or other information are received you will be promptly notified.

His mother hurried to call Jim's brothers and sisters with the devastating news. Questions of what it all meant stifled their conversations. They had no answers and there was no one to counsel them. Concern for Jim's welfare kept them perplexed – uncertain of what it all meant. "How long are we going to have to wait to know where he is?" Verda Lindsay cried out in anger. But there was no "help line" to call – thousands of others across the country received the same sad message and were in suspense also.

There was no helpful instruction of what to do – just wait. Apprehension for the welfare of their son became the daily companion of his parents. Valiantly they pushed aside any thought that he was dead. "Jim's tough," George assured his wife. "We just have to hope for the best."

A letter from the Adjutant General, dated 28 November 1944, followed that terse telegram – but it provided no helpful details and brought no relief to their anguish. It was addressed to his mother, whom he had designated as his contact person in case of an emergency:

Dear Mrs. Lindsay:

This letter is to confirm my recent telegram in which you were regretfully informed that your son, Technical Sergeant James B. Lindsay, 15,081,658, Air Corps, has been reported missing in action since 11 November 1944 over Italy.

I know that added distress is caused by failure to receive more information or details. Therefore, I wish to assure you that at any time additional information is received it will be transmitted to you without delay, and, if in the meantime no additional information is received, I will again communicate with you at the expiration of three months. Also, it is the policy of the Commanding General of the Army Air Forces upon receipt of the "Missing Air Crew report" to convey to you any details that might be contained in that report.

The term "missing in action" is used only to indicate that the whereabouts or status of an individual is not immediately known. It is not intended to convey the impression that the case is closed. I wish to emphasize that every effort is exerted continuously to clear up the status of our personnel. Under war conditions this is a difficult task, as you must readily realize. Experience has shown that many persons reported missing in action are subsequently reported as prisoners of war, but as this information is furnished by countries with which we are at war, the War Department is helpless to expedite such reports.

The personal effects of an individual missing overseas are held by his unit for a period of time and are then sent to the Effects Quartermaster, Kansas City, Missouri, for disposition as designated by the soldier.

Permit me to extend to you my heartfelt sympathy during this period of uncertainty.
Sincerely yours,

J. A. Ulio
Major General,
The Adjutant General

This letter was followed two days later by one from Jim's Commanding Officer of the Fifteenth Air Force:

My dear Mrs. Lindsay:

Important enemy installations in Salzburg, Austria, were bombed by Liberators of this air force on November 11, 1944. Your son, Technical Sergeant James B. Lindsay, 15081658, participated as the left waist gunner of his ship. As it failed to return to the base Jim and his crew have been missing in action since that date.

As observation was almost impossible over the target it is not known when Jim's ship left the formation. As no calls were received from the craft at any time we can do little but wait and hope for the best. Should details be received in the future the War Department will notify you immediately.

Jim's personal belongings have been assembled for shipment to the Effects Quartermaster, Army Effects Bureau, Kansas City, Missouri, who will in turn send them to the designated recipient.

The courage and efficiency, which Jim has displayed in numerous combat missions, has been officially recognized by the award of the Air Medal and two Oak Leaf Clusters.

Very Sincerely yours,

N. F. Twining
Major General, USA
Commanding

(An amazing sidelight of the Fifteenth's flight operations was its rescue and repatriation of aircrews shot down in enemy territory. No other Air Force Command had undertaken escape operations in so many countries. The Fifteenth returned 5,650 personnel by air, surface vessel and on foot through enemy lines. In more than 300 planned rescue operations, men were brought back safely from Tunisia, Italy, France, Switzerland, Greece, Albania, Bulgaria, Rumania, Hungary, Yugoslavia, Austria and Germany. Unfortunately, this did not apply to Sergeant Lindsay since the Air Force had no idea as to where he was.)

Dread and uncertainty blanketed the Lindsay household each day after the "missing in action" notices. Where might he be? They did there best to encourage one another – daily – that "missing in action" doesn't mean dead. Of concern to his mother was whether or not she needed to change the color of Jim's star in the rectangular armed services flag hanging in the front window of the house. Anxiously she asked her husband and sons, "Are we supposed to change his blue star? What color should it be for someone like Jim?"

"No, we're not going to change his star," her husband George asserted. "He'll be home."

Even so, Christmas, 1944, was a solemn occasion for the Lindsay family with no further news as to Jim's status – and with brothers Lawrence and Paul, now enlisted and away on their own Army assignments – and with brother-in-law Scott Johnson stationed in England with the Eighth Air Force. But the rest of the family gathered – three sisters and their children, along with Jim's three younger brothers. In spite of wartime rationing and shortages, Mom Lindsay managed to set out a feast of bounty and goodness, but there just wasn't much joy to go around.

Nor a week later did anyone make any special New Year's Eve plans. The uncertainty of Jim's whereabouts – whether he was living or dead – drew a dark pall over any idea of celebrating.

Indeed, the year seemed destined to end in darkness on December 31, with the sun already sinking beyond the horizon. But all of that changed when Western Union rang the front doorbell to deliver the following telegram sent from the Adjutant General with a time stamp of 4:31 pm:

Report just received through the International Red Cross states that your Son Technical Sergeant James B. Lindsay is a prisoner of war of the German Government. Letter of information follows from the Provost Marshall General.

Mrs. Lindsay - always tender of heart – sat down heavily on the edge of the maroon-colored sofa and burst into tears, holding the telegram lightly in her trembling hand. Slowly she relaxed and declared simply, "Well thank God for words of hope. At least we know he's alive." She had intended to stay up late to ring in the New Year. Instead she went to bed early, able to sleep soundly for the first time in a month. Though she did not know of the pitiable conditions under which he existed, at least she knew her son was alive – and that gave her a sense of security.

Unknown to her of course, was that later she would be able to understand exactly what he went through. On his first full day at Stalag Luft IV, as Sergeant Lindsay investigated his surroundings, he saw a brown, 5 by 7 notebook lying on a table. He looked around anxiously to see if anyone was watching – then slipped the book and a pencil into his pocket. Starting then he kept a daily diary of his experiences. Time would prove those pages to be of great historical significance. Of the more than a-half-million Prisoners of War, Technical Sergeant James B. Lindsay is the only one known to have maintained a chronicle of what he experienced. His detailed account of the horrors that the Germans put him and his comrades through, gives a vivid insight into the inhuman treatment prisoners of war endured.

The first notes he wrote of his imprisonment in describing the horrible conditions of Stalag IV were a faithful witness of undeserved torment. Cold and hungry, he nonetheless dutifully recorded specifics of what he and others bore up under. That alone was terrible, but the worse was yet to come.

Beginning in March 1945 - for 87 days – under the horrific conditions of what came to be known as The Black March, Lindsay faithfully maintained what is the only authentic eyewitness record of those three months of horror. Across the frozen countryside of Northern Germany, this 1945 German equivalent of the notorious and infamous 1942 Bataan Death March of the Japanese, was equally senseless and barbaric. Thankfully, Sergeant Lindsay faithfully noted the German design of misery against the prisoners. It is a lasting memorial for those who died in this senseless plot of the Germans – the courageous airmen of The Black March.

Chapter Four

STALAG IV – BEAST BARRACKS

Sergeant Lindsay was determined never to forget the difficult lessons he was learning as a Prisoner of War, hoping someday to be able to expose it all to others. So from his second day at Stalag IV – under the very noses of his captors – he began making daily entries into a personal diary. He thought that perhaps it could be used to bring retribution on the perpetrators of his unjustified suffering. As it turned out, the historical significance of this diary is inestimable - remarkable. Though many former POWs wrote brief accounts of their incarceration and terrible treatment at the hands of the Germans, his notes are the only glimpse into what men went through on a daily basis. At first glance, his initial entry was nothing earth shattering. But, when considering the circumstances of his situation, the down-to-earth simplicity and the natural way in which it was understated reveals a sly, Indiana farm boy's sense of humor. This inner fortitude would prove to be a help to sustain him in unbearable conditions – far worse than he had already experienced, or at that time could have imagined. Here he makes no mention of the unconscionable beating he had endured at the hands of the Commandant. Nor does he recount the privations during the arduous 1,000-mile trip across war torn Italy, Austria, Germany, and into Poland:

Dec. 5, 1944, I arrived at Stalag Luft #4. We were searched and then locked up. My new home is now room #2 in Bks #2 of C lager.

Dec. 6, 1944, We had two roll calls. I received a small amount of Red Cross to catch up with the rest of the fellows. The weather is really nasty. Wrote my first letter home.

Though he had been a prisoner for more than a month, this was his first experience with provisions from the Red Cross. What this organization brought to the prison camps became a necessary supplement to the diet of the Prisoners of War. In practicality it was vital, irreplaceable. It is unquestionably true that the watery soup, which was the mainstay of the German food offering, was totally lacking of any essential nutrients – and had nothing to bite into. To any normal, thinking human being, you would not give hungry men what you wouldn't even use to slop hogs. Often, unbelievably, there was more grass than potatoes in the soup. The only hope prisoners had for some bit of balance in their diet was through the Red Cross parcels. Some family members faithfully mailed packages from the United States, but these seldom got through because of pilfering along the way. So the Red Cross effort really made the difference between life and death for tens of thousands of Prisoners of War. Consistently, tirelessly, throughout the years of war, more than 13,500 volunteers assembled 27 million parcels in New York City, Philadelphia, Chicago, and St. Louis for shipment to prison camps in Europe. Almost nothing went to the Pacific prison camps because of a total lack of cooperation from the Japanese. But the Germans were different in this regard - they allowed a significant amount of this humanitarian assistance to get through. Amazingly, in the last year of the war, German U-boats did nothing to hinder nine Red Cross ships – fully lighted and without escort – to pass safely across the Atlantic from the United States to Europe to deliver this desperately needed aid.

For practical purposes the Red Cross boxes were standardized, using a format of 10" x 10" x 4 ½ ". This made it possible to maximize the valuable and limited shipping space. Each box was filled with non-perishable items. Normally a parcel would contain small amounts of such things as tins of liver pate, coffee, corned beef, oleomargarine, biscuits, orange juice concentrate, cheese, and salmon or tuna fish, along with prunes, raisins, sugar, dried milk, a chocolate bar, cigarettes, and soap. To be sure, in such small amounts, it offered just a taste of something good. But in face of the destitute situation of the prisoners, often on the point of starvation, even a little bit of something good was an encouragement. It also helped to keep hope alive, knowing that there was someone – some unknown person back home who cared.

Noting that he "received a small amount" underscores the extreme shortages that prisoners endured. Neither that first day, nor at any time after, did Jim or any other prisoner ever receive a whole Red Cross parcel to himself. The supply was limited and demand limitless. Typically 4 to 6 POWS would divide the contents of one small box; and admirably the sharing was accomplished without argument. Though the boxes were intended for Prisoners of War, they contained delicacies to which German soldiers did not have access, so pilfering was widespread. The Red Cross did what it could to confirm delivery to the prisoners, but accurate accountability within the framework of a brutal war was not possible. Some of the items, however, did wind up in German possession by legitimate means. The prisoners would exchange with guards they trusted on a system of trade. Cigarettes for fresh eggs headed the bartering list.

It is impossible to calculate how many men were saved from total starvation because of the few calories they received because of the efforts of the International Red Cross.

Yes, Sergeant Lindsay did send a letter home. When it arrived in Kokomo a month later, his mother and father were both distressed and pleased at the same time. "At least he's alive," his mother said. "I know this is his handwriting. But there is no sense to what he wrote – the German censors have blotted out nearly every other word."

"Damned Germans," George Lindsay responded. "What could he have written on this little scrap of paper that would hurt them?"

Looking at the crumpled aerogramme with its German imprinted stamp, his youngest brother asked excitedly, "Can I take it to school to show Mrs. William's class?"

His mother wasted no time in getting to the post office the next day to get the prescribed *"Kriegsgefangenenpost"* – Prisoner of War Post. The fold-over mailer was free and the postage fee was a whopping six cents. Without leaving the post office she quickly wrote him a message of love and encouragement. Affixing Jim's prisoner of war number – 4836 – she dropped it in the outgoing mail.

But as a loving mother she was far from finished. She asked a clerk, "What about packages to my son who is a Prisoner of War in Germany? What can I send him? How long does it take to get there?"

"Hard to tell," he responded. "For POWs we give it priority - but once the Germans get it, who knows? Anyway, here is a suggested list of items that could be helpful to him."

She studied the list and went immediately to the store to buy two pairs of socks, briefs, and t-shirts; 3 bars of soap, a pound of coffee, and a carton of cigarettes. (Even though she knew that her son didn't smoke, she had heard enough about the war to know that they were a handy means of trade.) She went home to bake her famous Prune Cake. Because of its high-moisture content she was counting on it to stay fresh for a month or more. The next morning she packed everything together and walked back to the post office (with wartime gas rationing so strict she and her husband had given up their car) – content that she had done all she could for the moment.

Unfortunately she was the only one in the family blessed by sending that box. It never got to her son.

Dec. 7, 1944 - Three years ago today we entered this war. Got German coffee this morning. After roll call we got raisins and cigs from Red Cross rations. Later in the afternoon we got another jam and salmon through one from R.C.

Dec. 8, 1944 - Stayed in bed until last moment, then had to rush to get out to parade on time. Nothing new.

Dec. 9, 1944 – We had an inspection of silverware, bowls and cups. Some had to stay out at roll call for about two hours. I just about froze, as did the rest of the fellows. My feet stayed numb most of the morning.

Most German Prisoner of War camps were acknowledged to have observed the letter of the law. But some were a world unto themselves; isolated kingdoms in far off places, where men of cruelty and ill will could do their worst. Unfortunately for Jim Lindsay, Stalag Luft IV was that kind of a camp. Secluded in a forested area in a corner of Poland, it was far away from the prying eyes of civilization and the rule of law. Long, unnecessary hours of standing in the frigid air of the Polish winter were not unusual – this time under the ridiculous pretense of checking dishware. Such events were not merely circumstantial. Rather it was all a designed plan to add as much misery as possible to the prisoners, while seemingly conducting legitimate procedures for the good of the camp. The War Crimes Trial briefs filed immediately after the war, however, cited four officers of Stalag Luft IV- Richard Pickhardt, Aribert Bombach, Reinhardt Fahnert, and Hans Schmidt – as being responsible for an organized reign of terror, lasting from March 1944 to May 1945. Most heinous of the crimes for which they were cited was the wanton execution of four unarmed American airmen under mysterious circumstances.

Prisoners made up nicknames, to be used among themselves, for officers and guards for whom they had no respect. It was a clever way to declare these perpetrators of evil with titles of disapproval. "The Mad Captain" (Pickhardt) and "Big Stoop" (Hans Schmidt) were two of the most notorious for blatant cruelty. Colonel Bombach – "Snaggletooth" – had total control over the camp. He aggressively exerted himself at every opportunity possible – as with his first encounter knockdown of Sergeant Lindsay. Surrounded by a cadre of dedicated Nazis, he executed authority as if this were a penal colony. He had one rule: there would be no escapes from Stalag Luft IV. Consequently, the behavior of the guards was unrestrained – he openly encouraged brutal and harsh disciplinary measures – knockdowns with rifle butts by guards were repeated on a daily basis.

Even though the prisoners organized themselves and elected a camp leader – an American, Sergeant Francis Paules – Bombach refused to recognize him and never consulted with him. (Such an attitude makes the former television series "Hogan's Heroes"; residing at Stalag 13, seem like a really sick joke.) The enormous pride Bombach had in his rank and position prohibited him from talking to a mere sergeant as an equal. Besides that, he detested the very thought of conferring with a lice-infested prisoner. To the contrary, he often openly boasted of his hatred for these miserable men who were responsible for so much destruction in Germany.

Another American, Captain Henry James Wynsen from Youngstown, Ohio, was one consistent impediment to Bombach's authoritarian rule. Because of his medical training he was kept with the noncommissioned prisoners to serve as a "show piece" – supposedly as an adviser and helper. He had been a prisoner of the Germany Army from November 1942. Endlessly he continually pushed the Commandant to improve conditions for the men, but to no avail. In spite of Wynsen's rank, Bombach paid no attention to him. He considered himself alone as the sole authority for the conduct of the camp and he despised any input from those he considered lower than slime. A growth in their numbers became a major problem for the prisoners. Though the four prison compounds at Stalag IV had been built to accommodate approximately 1600 men each, with new arrivals coming in daily that count was pushed to as many as 2500. After the war Wynsen testified, "The total camp strength by January 1945 was approximately 10,000 prisoners. Rooms in barracks were at least fifty percent overcrowded. Men were required to sleep on floors and tables. The barracks were inadequately ventilated because of blackout regulations prohibiting the opening of windows and doors.

He further affirmed that while he was at Stalag Luft IV, "No American or British soldier was ever issued any German clothing, socks, underwear, etc. It was the policy of German officers and enlisted men, at this camp to purposely hinder the issuance of Red Cross clothing to American Prisoners of War. Generally speaking, the prisoners' clothing was in bad condition. They were very short of underclothing due to the fact that in some instances shirts from the Red Cross consignments had not been distributed. In this connection it must be mentioned that in many cases, and especially in Camp A, German workmen were met, who wore American effects.

Dec. 10, 1944 – To get this morning off to a flying start we received hot water from the mess hall to make coffee with after roll call. We received RC rations, ½ can of milk, ¾ can of coffee, ½ box of sugar (¼ lb), a full "D" ration chocolate bar and later on ½ can of Spam. We had regular army "C" rations with a few potatoes added. It came through the mess hall and tasted pretty good.

Dec. 11, 1944 – G. I. Woolen gloves came in and I was lucky enough to draw a pair. The whole room peeled potatoes (a basket full). For dinner we had something they call soup – actually I think that it was boiled grass. The weather is getting colder. Took a bath today. RC rations came in. We got cigarettes and cocoa.

As incredible as it may sound, the Germans really did use grass as an ingredient in soup – not only for Prisoners of War – but also for the general population. They tried to disguise it as a supplement to various legumes. As the war was drawing to a close, food supplies were short for everyone in war torn Germany – the military, civilians – and at the bottom of the list, Prisoners of War. In his diary Lindsay seldom makes mention of the daily bread ration that was usually offered as a slice with a bit of butter or jam on it in the morning. Perhaps he often ignored the bread ration because, like the soup, it also was counterfeited. The contents of this hard to swallow "bread" was made by following a strict, nationally ordered recipe of 50% bruised rye grain, 20% diced sugar beets, 20% tree flour (sawdust), and 10% minced leaves or straw.

His notation that he took a bath is a significant exaggeration on his part – more of that sly Hoosier humor. Having been always meticulous in his hygiene and appearance it had been especially difficult for him at that time to have gone for more than a month without a "bath". But bathing – in the normal meaning of the word – at Stalag IV was not possible. There were no showers or tubs in any of the four compounds. So his "bath" was only possible by pouring cold water into a bowl – the same bowl he and others used for food – and using a cloth to cleanse each part of the body. Normally a bath also implies the use of soap, but there was none available.

Also there were no adequate facilities in the compounds for the relief of body fluids and waste. Each barracks had a two-hole latrine for 240 POWs to be used at night. For daytime used only, each lager (compound) had two open-air latrines with 20 holers back to back with urinals. No one lingered long at the toilets because the odor was horrific. To drain the stagnant pits the Germans made use of Russian POWs, from another camp, who spread the sludge as fertilizer on fields outside the camp area.

In order to get the full impact of Sergeant Lindsay's diary one has to look with understanding at the significance of the fractions he used for the food items he received. For someone who is always at the point of starvation, food – the very thought of food – becomes an overwhelming preoccupation. A thoughtful reader soon begins to feel the hunger pangs of the prisoners – by noting the minimal grams and ounces of the food items received. Remember, when he writes about cans or boxes he is referring to tiny containers – small ones – like the bag of peanuts given to passengers on an airline flight. In the entire diary there is never a mention of fresh fruit or vegetables (other than potatoes and carrots) – they were totally nonexistent for prisoners. Consequently, illnesses that result from a lack of fresh produce were rampant at Stalag IV. Jim's listing day-after day became for him a boring litany of what little he had at his disposal to keep from starving. There was never the joy of biting into a piece of fresh fruit.

Dec. 12, 1944 – (Tuesday) Don't know what time it started but last night it began and this morning when we got up it was snowing to beat the band. A lot of snowballing went on at roll call. Dinner was good (thick potato soup) Supper at 1900 – spuds with corned beef added. Here's hoping that the rumor that came in today is true – 10,000 Christmas parcels have arrived.

Dec. 13, 1944 – This morning at roll call the German Captain was really mad because some of the fellows were smoking in ranks. Most of the ground is covered with ice. The correct story on the RC Christmas parcels is 6980 – a few of the fellows received theirs. Nate Carews found out that he is a father (baby girl). Sauerkraut – potatoes for dinner (hard to eat). Corned beef and potatoes for supper. The contents of the Christmas parcels look pretty good.

Dec. 14, 1944 – snowed this morning for about a half and hour. Rec. ½ box prunes, ¼ box raisins, 1 can jam, 1 box K-2 biscuits, 1¾ oz can of butter, ½ can of pate.

Dec. 15, 1944 – Last night we all just about froze – our coal ration is very small and the stove is a very poor excuse. We are still sleeping on the floor but expect bunks soon. German coffee this morning and soup for dinner.

Plain boiled spuds for supper. We have 22 men in our little room and they have a hard time trying to gather around the stove to keep warm.

The weather for that part of Poland is similar to that of Central New England, with plenty of cold temperatures and heavy snow in the winter months. The barracks in which the men were housed had been put up in a hasty manner during the previous summer with no thought of weatherproofing, so the outside temperature had little difficulty in forcing its way inside. To ward off the cold, the coal allowance the Germans had for each little room was ridiculously insufficient – only ten little briquettes a day, which amounted to less than a pound. It was an impossible struggle to try to get warm with 22 men trying to gain a space around a stove with only a three-foot circumference. Nor could they overcome the bitter cold with more clothing. The Germans provided them with nothing. For most of them, what clothing they had was the same attire they had at the time of their capture – and with the passing of time that was woefully inadequate and in a bad, raggedy condition. This was significantly true of underclothing that was never replaced. Though it was documented that a British Red Cross consignment of shirts arrived at the camp, they were never distributed to the prisoners. Instead, as Wynsen had observed, especially in Camp A, German workmen wore the garments intended for the POWs. The only additional clothing Jim Lindsay received during his eight months as a Prisoner of War was the pair of woolen gloves he got on December 11.

Dec. 16, 1944 – Snowed again last night and is really cold. RC rations came in – 1 can milk, 1 can of coffee, ½ box of sugar (¼ lb). The Germans had knife inspection this morning at parade. The rest of the day passed as usual. For supper we had C-ration stew with spuds and it was sure tasty. Just goes to show how being a POW can change the taste of things.

As a relatively poor Indiana farm boy, Jim had grown up on a diet full of potatoes. Home grown "spuds" were cheap and plentiful – and Verda Lindsay had at least a dozen ways to make them truly "tasty". Indeed, by this time, hunger had counterfeited – distorted – his taste buds.

Dec. 17, 1944 – I am splitting rations with Hump. He got up first this morning and fixed us a cup of hot chocolate (very good Bill). We had a different Capt. at roll call today. We received raisins, chocolate, 2 pks of cigarettes and a box of K-2 biscuits. Played a little poker today and won 16pks. They sure make good trading material.

This date also marked even worse conditions for other Prisoners of War of the Germans. Unfortunately, not everyone who was captured made it to a camp. In the course of the war there were some horrific atrocities committed by both sides. Because of battle conditions, those in charge often made hasty and terrible decisions. This was compounded for the Germans, as an aggressive attitude against the enemy became a part of their marching orders. As the tide of the conflict turned decisively in favor of the Allied forces, Adolph Hitler made the already bitter methods of the most ardent Nazis the official strategy for all officers and men. In advance of what proved to be the last significant offensive of the Germans – which resulted in the "Battle of the Bulge" – he demanded that his soldiers must be especially brutal in order to intensify fear in the minds of the enemy. It was made clear by the instructions from Berlin that no mercy was to be given to the other side. That mind-set brought about one of the worst atrocities of the War. It occurred at Malmedy, France during the Ardennes Offensive.

At about noon on December 17, 1944, the Combat Group of the 1st Panzer Division, commanded by SS Major Joachim Peiper arrived at the crossroads at Baugnes near the town of Malmedy. It was a cold, blustery day. Snow was falling, adding to the deep pack that was already there. Unexpectedly, the Germans encountered a company of U. S. troops – Battery B of the 285th Field Artillery Observation Battalion from the U. S. 7th Armored Division – which had advanced beyond its own battle lines. A fierce, but brief, firefight ensued. With pinpoint accuracy the German Panzers blew up the lead and rear trucks of the American 29-truck convoy. Having only rifles and small arms with which to defend themselves – compared to the heavy firepower of the German tanks – the situation for the Americans was obviously hopeless and the officer in charge, Lieutenant Virgil Lary, decided to surrender.

After being disarmed and searched by the SS, the prisoners were herded into an open field. There they were joined by other Americans who had been captured earlier – 131 in all.

SS Major Peiper, strictly following orders from headquarters, had made it clear to his men already that there was to be no mercy shown to the enemy – and to take no prisoners. Thus the die was cast. When he moved on with his column, he left behind two Mark IV tanks with their escorts to guard the GIs. After only a matter of minutes, suddenly and without a word of warning, the Germans opened fire with machine guns on the unarmed men. As soon as the first shots rang out, panic ran rampant among the unsuspecting Americans. Instantly dozens of the prisoners fell dead in the hail of bullets. Some men instinctively ran and ducked for cover in the nearby woods, but the vast majority of them were gunned down where they stood, crumpling to the ground. Some feigned death, thinking that would save them, and fell prone on the ground. However, SS troops walked across the field, inspecting the torn and bleeding bodies. Any who were found to be still alive were promptly shot through the head. In that fashion, at least 20 were summarily executed. Regular army soldiers also responded to groans from among the fallen Americans and cruelly crushed their heads with the butt of their rifles – not wasting another bullet.

The two tanks then rumbled on, leaving behind the bloodied bodies in the scene of carnage.

Incredibly, 43 men survived the massacre and slipped back to American forces in the west. But no one from the U. S. Command made any attempt the retrieve the bodies of the slain men. For a month the exposed bodies of the dead were left subject to the elements and wild animals. It was not until January 15, 1945 that American forces got back to the scene to uncover the frozen, snow-covered corpses of the 88 victims of the vicious brutality.

Jim Lindsay, of course, had no knowledge of this mass murder until after the war. But he was able to readily identify with such warped cruelty because of his own experiences. What he could never understand, however, was why? How could men be made to stoop to such extreme barbaric behavior? Though he had suffered through it experientially, he could never explain it – other than that the Germans he encountered had their inner spirit twisted beyond what God had intended.

Dec. 18, 1944 – Monday – Breakfast in bed, now that's not bad at all. It was fixed by Bill and consisted of raisins, biscuits and milk fixed as a cereal, also a cup of hot chocolate. Sauerkraut for dinner. The whole room peeled spuds. Lights out at 20:30.

It is notable throughout the diary that "breakfast" is seldom mentioned. Back home on the farm in Indiana breakfast had been a big deal – a man had to have a hearty helping of food to be prepared for a hard day's work. Though the Germans expected the prisoners to get up bright and early for roll call, they seldom if ever provided a food incentive. Jim and his buddies had to improvise for themselves.

Dec. 19, 1944 – We received jam from the Germans. Dinner consisted of dry greens and potatoes – plain spuds for supper. R. C. rations came in – 1 can of butter and ½ can of cheese.

Dec. 20, 1944 – Barley cereal for dinner – it was good. Played a little poker and came out about even.

Dec. 21, 1944 – Thursday – This morning the mess hall gave out that vulgar tasting German coffee. Some towels came in from the R. C., but I didn't get one. Jam and salmon also came in.

Dec. 22, 1944 – After parade Bks #2 was on detail so I went over to another Bks and played some bridge. Plain potatoes for supper. The Christmas parcels have come into the lager and will be given out Sunday morning.

Dec. 23, 1944 – About the only new development that has come this way in a long time happened today. We have finally gotten beds. They are double deckers and 3 men wide. Putting them in was an all day job.

Dec. 24, 1944 – Sunday – "Christmas Eve" we got our Christmas parcels and they are really nice. We had barley cereal for dinner. The Germans are letting us stay outside until midnight under special parole – also they gave each room three table bowls. The Christmas parcels consisted of – 12 oz. Turkey, 6 oz jam, 8 oz honey, 4 oz dates, 2 fruit bars (2 oz each), 1 can of candy, 1 can of fruit, a box of tea, 12 bullion cubes, 1 can of cheese, 1 lb of plum pudding, 1 can of Viennese sausage (4 oz), 1 can of deviled ham, 1 can of cheese, 1 can of butter, deck of cards, a pipe, wash cloth, 4 packs of gum, 3 packs of cigarettes, a pack of tobacco, and two pictures and a game.

Dec. 25, 1944 – Monday – "Christmas" We got barley cereal for dinner and plain potatoes for supper. All the fellows are in a happy state of mind and they are eating like mad. The turkey was sure good. Today was really hard on the stomach. My thoughts are all of home and here is hoping that they have a nice Christmas at home.

Sergeant Lindsay was able to maintain such a healthy frame of mind because he constantly was thinking of life beyond the compound. He never lost sight of his goal to have strawberry shortcake for his birthday back home in Indiana. Whether as a Prisoner of War or as an inmate in a penal institution, a man can become "stir crazy" if he only thinks of the deprivations of his incarceration. Remembering that there is life beyond the walls, beyond the barbed wire, is necessary for mental well being. Because he maintained a positive attitude and a determination to live as normal a life as possible under what really were impossible conditions, Jim was an inspiration and a help to his buddies.

But, as mentioned previously, Christmas was not a joyous occasion for his family back in Kokomo, Indiana. There had been no word of him since November. The "Missing in Action" notices were not great harbingers of hope, but rather stirred up unanswerable questions. Certainly his mother – if she had known about it – would have heartily thanked all those Red Cross volunteers who had worked so tirelessly to give her son such a happy Christmas. (In order to get the boxes to the men in December, the volunteers had begun putting them together in July.) But Jim's hope for a "nice Christmas" for those back home just wasn't possible. Their relief, by news about him, was still a week away.

Dec. 26, 1944 – Most of today was taken up recuperating from the results of yesterday's eating. So it's so long to a "Merry Christmas".

Dec. 27, 1944 – Things are back to normal again and we are again having one, two roll calls a day. Went to a musical at the R. C. room – was really good.

Dec. 28, 1944 – Two roll calls. Had songs with English R. C. – vegetables – for supper we had plain spuds.

De c. 29, 1944 – Last night it snowed – the most snow we have had yet. We had "buckshot" peas for dinner. R. C. Rations came in – a can of milk, ½ can of coffee, ½ box of sugar. Supper consisted of potatoes with salmon added.

Dec. 30, 1944 – Sat. (close to New Year) the wind was really blowing at roll call this morning. More R. C. rations – ½ can of coffee, 1 B-bar, and 5 packs of cigarettes.

Dec. 31, 1944 – The snow is several in. deep and the snowballs flew during the entire day. The room peeled spuds today. I helped open Spam at the mess hall.

By the time 1944 came to an end, Jim Lindsay had settled into some meaningful relationships with men in barracks two. They were all keenly aware that they were stuck together in a horrible situation, which was not likely to get better. But the way they supported one another and shared what little they had was remarkable – selfishness was rare, if ever at all. This type of unity helped Jim maintain an optimistic attitude and he was thankful for each of them. He was determined to live through anything the Germans set against him.

Back home in Indiana, the long month of agony – waiting for word of his whereabouts – finally ended for his family. Of course, they knew nothing of his torment, or where he was exactly; but they could rejoice that he was alive because they knew of his stalwart stamina. After New Years, his mom took his youngest brother and went to see Pastor Ruby. Though, at the time, the family was not churchgoers, she knew she needed spiritual guidance so she turned to the man in whom Jim had such confidence. The Pastor helped her gain a positive outlook, in spite of all the negative news coming out of Germany. She prayed a lot. Though there was a glimmer of hope as the New Year began, there were months of uncertainty ahead.

Meanwhile for Jim and his fellow prisoners matters worsened with each succeeding day in 1945. His diary chronicles a steady decline in the German's ability to provide any sufficient supply of food – or anything else – for the prisoners.

And for the Germany Army, on all fronts, the war effort was deteriorating steadily. Though they were in retreat, they nevertheless fought on.

Chapter Five
STALAG IV – A COLD HARD WINTER

Part of the reason for the miserable conditions at Stalag IV was that the Germans had hastily slapped it together in June of 1944 to transfer prisoners away from the rapidly collapsing Eastern Front. They had given no consideration for comfort – just confinement. Then, because of a steady arrival of additional prisoners, no time or thought was given to improve the drafty wooden barracks. This overcrowding was especially complicated when a large consignment of prisoners were dumped into the camp. This came about as a direct consequence of the steady advance of Soviet troops battling from the east. So, in order to maintain control of its prisoners, the Germans were forced to close Stalag VI at Hydekrug in East Prussia, moving the men to Stalag IV. This transfer of approximately 2400 American airmen was brutal and forceful and under unnecessarily horrible conditions. It was obvious from the conduct of the transfer that the intention of the Germans was to make the relocation as unbearable as possible for the Americans. The first stage of the move was by ship from Memel, Lithuania, across a southern portion of the Baltic Sea to the German port of Swinemunde. The entire contingent of prisoners was jammed into the cargo holds of two dilapidated coastal coal tramp steamers, with no consideration to provide anything for hygienic necessities. Worse yet, while being tossed about in the duressing darkness during the five-day passage, the airmen were on starvation rations – no food or water was provided.

It would have been a total tragedy if the ships had sunk because no life preservers were available.

Upon disembarking, the famished, weary, and filthy prisoners were chained like animals in cattle cars for the duration of the second leg of the journey - a train ride to the station at Kiefeheide, Poland. Still no food or water was given. The soon-to-become-infamous Colonel Aribert Bombach, who had been second in command at Stalag VI, was now assigned as the Commandant at Stalag IV. He had given harsh orders that the prisoners were to be forced to move double time on the four-kilometer march from the station to the camp. During that run, the guards wielded rifle butts and bayonets freely, cursing loudly as they did so. It was a chaotic scene with guard dogs barking and snapping at the legs of the defenseless Americans. If a prisoner fell down from exhaustion, a German soldier would jab his bayonet into the man's body mercilessly until he got back on his feet. Consequently, some men had multiple wounds. Because of the forced speed – and the weakness from food deprivation - even the strongest men stumbled along through the oppressive heat of the Polish summer. It wasn't possible for the men to keep hold of their baggage. The few meager possessions they had managed to accumulate at Stalag VI were dropped along the way and confiscated by the German guards.

Major Gruber - who had been Security Officer at Stalag VI was chosen to be Lager Officer for Compound A at Stalag IV. He was in charge of the pathetic Baltic boat ride and set the pace for the run up the road. He was of stocky build at 170 pounds and only 5' 8". He wore a patch on his left eye and had thin straight blond hair. The prisoners put together several derogatory names for him to fit particular situations – "Hollywood", "Medals", and "Snake-Eyes". This simple act of disrespect for the guards was at the same time a unifying factor for the prisoners – they were standing together against evil forces in about the only way they could.

The intentional, wanton cruelty against the transferred prisoners continued even after arrival at the camp. There the prisoners were struck with gun butts and subjected to disparaging insults. Many suffered additional bayonet wounds - even after being secured behind the barbed wire fences. *Hauptman* (Captain) Sommers, chief medical officer for Stalag IV, dutifully – but superficially - examined 200 dog bites and bayonet wounds and diagnosed all of them as sunstroke. He refused to give any treatment or medication; open wounds were left untended. Aged 50, standing 5' 10", with dark hair, graying at the temples, Sommers was continually unsympathetic to suffering on the part of the prisoners. Little wonder then that the men had to be extremely ill before going to the infirmary, since no significant treatment was ever given.

Fortunately, occasionally, there was some conscientious leadership among the Germans. Much to his credit, one unnamed German officer accompanying the prisoners protested very strongly to headquarters against the harsh physical treatment. This brought about the need for an official inquiry from higher authorities. After investigations by the Minister of Aviation – which was only a charade - it was determined that the distance from the station to the camp could easily be covered in 25 minutes. Therefore, since the prisoners were young and athletic men, the marching pace was not considered too fast. Besides, for reasons of security, the distance had to be covered rapidly – a slow pace might have favored escapes. It was noted that the guards were only doing their duty, having been ordered to be severe towards stubbornness or provocative behavior on part of the prisoners. On the basis of the authoritative witness of the German troop doctor (Sommers) it was concluded that if injuries had occurred, they were only very light in nature.

It is true that none of the prisoners died from their wounds that day, but those who endured the experience estimated that more than one hundred had been bayoneted during the course of the run to the Stalag.

Colonel Bombach had little say as to who was assigned from the German Army to his new command at Stalag IV. With the war going poorly for the Germans, only the dregs of the military were available for prison guard duty. Nonetheless, Bombach, who was a member of the Nazi Party and had been a pre-war agent in France, made do with what he had, and gave unlimited authority to the most cruel of the officers under his command. Captain of the Guard Pickhardt headed the list of fanatical Nazis at Stalag IV. He had been in charge of the run from the train station and continually abused prisoners physically, also pilfering their belongings and supplies. Aged 45 and only 5' 3", with a reddish complexion, he looked bulky – and even dwarfish - in his white airman's coat. Prisoners had a number of nicknames for him – "Ice Cream Man", "Mad Captain", "Butcher of Berlin".

It was under such men of low moral character that Sergeant Lindsay began a new year of imprisonment in the frozen wastelands of Northern Poland.

Jan 1, 1945 – "New Year's Day" Last night true to form the old year was put out and the new year in with a lot of noise. Roll call and snowballs.

Jan 2, 1945 – The weather is cold but nice compared to what we have had. The mess hall gave out hot chocolate in the afternoon (from ERC). The potatoes for evening supper had corned beef added.

Jan 3, 1945 – We peeled spuds today. The weather is really nasty, the ice and snow has begun to melt and it's raining. The RC rations were ½ box of sugar, 1 box of K-2 crackers and 2 oz of chocolate. The ice pond that was being made has gone with the wind because of the change in temps.

Jan 4, 1945 – Thursday – The mess hall gave out Jerry coffee this morning. The ground outside is certainly a mess – ice and snow melted with a little dirt added. We had some kind of a Jerry Day concoction. Received 1 can of salmon and 1 can of jam.

Now that he was mixed together with a few British airmen, Lindsay was quick to pick up some of their lingo. He especially appreciated the term "Jerry". This derogatory name for a German had originated during the First World War. It was also a colloquial term used by common people in England to denote "a chamber pot". Lindsay was quick to appreciate the significance of the derision and he used the term frequently.

Jan 5, 1945 – We got pate from Red Cross rations. The room peeled carrots. I played bridge almost all day.

Jan 6, 1945 – Jerry coffee from mess hall. Dinner was carrots, potatoes and German corned beef. Right after roll call RC rations came in – milk, ½ box of sugar, ½ can of coffee. Plain spuds for supper.

Jan 7, 1945 – Hot water from the mess hall this morning. The room peeled potatoes. Barley cereal at 10:30. Eleven fellows went home for repatriation. This morning received 2 oz MM, 2 oz of chocolate, 1 box prunes, 3 pks cigarettes, soap, vit tablets, also ½ can of Spam. Supper was just potatoes (I put Spam and butter in them).

He writes here about "repatriation" but that is a misnomer. To repatriate literally means to return to one's fatherland. What evidently happened in this case was a "prisoner exchange", which was itself rather rare during the course of the war because it required cooperation on both sides. Because of bitter distrust from both sides such exchanges were seldom accomplished.

Repatriation of prisoners even after the war was a boondoggle of major proportions on the part of the American Government. The American military became so focused on punishing the really big German bad guys that it paid little attention to what happened to the surviving Prisoners of War. In 1945 more than 20,000 American POWs were "liberated" by the Russian Army as it marched triumphantly across Germany. But tragically they were never repatriated. Instead they were carted off to the Soviet Union where they lived the rest of their lives in the Russian gulag – in forced slave labor – never to be heard of again. Their cases were never pursued. Rather, they were abandoned, evidently forgotten by the American military. That left their families with a lasting and empty "missing in action" notification – never a closure to their grief.

The dismal fate of Russian POWs was on an even broader scale. Here too the government of the United States was complicit in a tragedy of enormous human suffering. At the Yalta Conference on February 15, 1945, American President Franklin Roosevelt and British Prime Minister Winston Churchill entered into a secret agreement with Joseph Stalin concerning Russian prisoners of war. It required that any Red Army Prisoners of War the United States and Great Britain might rescue from the Germans would be returned – forcibly if necessary - to the cruel clutches of Stalin. At the close of the war, though liberated by American and British forces, more than a million Russian POWs – though pleading for asylum - were repatriated against their will back to the Soviet Union. Once in the hands of the Soviet Army, most of them were summarily executed on the charge of treason for having surrendered in the first place. Untold thousands of others were sent to dismal camps in Siberia, where most of them perished under the harsh treatment of forced labor.

In like manner, the Soviets also were notably cruel to Nazi prisoners who fell into their clutches. This was demonstrated most graphically after the decisive Battle of Stalingrad – during which 200,000 German soldiers and nearly a half million Russians – military and civilians - died during the course of eight grueling months of close-quarter combat. For the last four months of that miserable struggle, which ended in mid-February 1944, the soldiers on both sides also had to battle freezing temperatures and heavy snows. Meanwhile, with tons of American aide, the Soviets made a massive increase in its forces and armaments behind the lines of battle. In spite of this, Hitler gave direct orders to General Friedrich Paulus, that the German Army must stand its ground and not retreat from the banks of the Volga River. It was a ridiculous command and resulted in a major turning point in the war – it resulted in the effective elimination of German strength on the Eastern Front. Against impossible odds – and without food and ammunition – the Germans were faced with a humiliating failure. For the first time in history a German General surrendered to a Russian. In doing so, General Paulus delivered 91,000 prisoners to the Red Army, including 21 generals. Most of these men were sick and starving as a result of having been cut off for months from German supply lines. But surrendering did them no good, 86,000 of them died under pitiless conditions of slave labor. Paulus was one of the few who survived. He returned to Germany seven years after the war in 1952. Finally, in 1955, on a plea from German Chancellor Konrad Adenauer to the Soviet Politburo, the last of these men - only 5,000 - that had survived their imprisonment were repatriated.

To be sure, such inhumane treatment was not one-sided. During the course of the War the Axis Powers – primarily the Germans - took 5.7 million Soviet soldiers prisoner. Of these 3.3 million – or 57.5 % - died at the hands of their captors.

In contrast, American, British and Canadian POWs fared better. Approximately four million American military personnel landed in Europe to help defeat the Nazi menace. Of these, the Germans took

232,000 of them as prisoners. During their incarceration 8,348 - 3.5% of them - died.

During Stalag IV's seven months of operation, many men died from various illnesses. But more tragically there were four American airmen who were known to have been shot to death – Aubry Teague, George Walker, Walter Getsey, and Walter Niles. Though it was never proven who actually committed the murders, Captain Voltz was on duty when Sergeants Niles and Walker were shot. Voltz was aged 45, 5' 5", 200 lbs, and bald. He wore tortoise shell rimmed glasses, had gold teeth, and walked with hands behind his back. He also was in charge of guards on the Baltic boat ride. Another officer, Oberfeldwebel Fahnert, was implicated in the Teague shooting. He also had a key role in the forced run from the train station to the camp. He was aged 50, thin, 6' tall; sharp features, and wore horn-rimmed glasses. The prisoners dubbed him "Iron Cross".

Jan 8, 1945 – Hot water from mess hall. No guards at roll call. Jerry corned beef soup for dinner. I did my washing this morning. 2 pks cigarettes, ½ box sugar, 1 box crackers, ½ can corned beef, ½ can coffee. Super was C-rations with spuds.

Jan 9, 1945 – Hot water from mess hall. Roll call about 10:30. It started snowing and continued all day. Carrot soup for dinner. No RC rations. C-rations stew for supper.

Jan 10, 1945 – Hot water from mess hall. The room peeled potatoes. RC rations of butter, cheese and 1 D bar came in. Dinner was carrots and potatoes stew – snow continued until about 16:30. We had plain spuds for supper.

Jan 11, 1945 – The usual two roll calls. Jerry Coffee this morning and Red Cross – 1 D bar, 1 can of sardines, ½ can salmon (tuna fish), 1 can of jam. Plain spuds for dinner.

Jan 12, 1945 – Jerry coffee – roll call – the ice and snow melted during the night and the ground is really a mess. Potato soup for supper and our room got the extra ½ bucket.

Jan 13, 1945 – Hot water from mess hall. Received milk, coffee, and ½ box of sugar from RC rations. The room peeled potatoes. I won 3 pks of cigarettes playing poker.

Jan 14, 1945 – ½ can c-beef and ½ can Spam for RC rations. Barley cereal for supper and was it good.

Jan 15, 1945 – (Monday) Hot water from mess hall – roll call. My side of the room peeled 2 buckets of spuds. Hurley was appointed camp RC rep for food. Sgt Farrell received a big parcel from home. He came down last July 12, 1944 – they were lucky.

At last some measure of honor was given to the men murdered at Malmedy, France. On January 15, 1945, 88 twisted and frozen bodies of massacred American soldiers were dug out of the snow and debris left from the day of their slaughter. Before being interred in a military cemetery, autopsies showed that 20 had died by a bullet to the back of the head and a half-dozen had crushed skulls – apparently caused by rifle butt blows.

But would anyone ever pay the penalty for this crime?

With this breakthrough by the United States Army, the Battle of the Bulge was finally over. From that point on the Western Front was in continual decline for the Germans. A rush to the Rhine River was the next focus, with an urgent, ultimate goal to beat the Soviets to Berlin.

Jan 16, 1945 – Hot water from mess hall – roll call as usual – after dinner RC rations – 1 D bar and 1 can of cheese. Our bed peeled a bucket of carrots.

Jan 17, 1945 – Jerry coffee – regular blizzard most of the day. RC rations – salmon. Supper plain potatoes (extra ½ pail).

Jan 18, 1945 – same old routine – Jam and pate from RC. Bridge tournament started in the bks. Got Jerry jam from Germans.

Jan 19, 1945 – Usual routine – Jerry coffee. N RC rations. Spuds were peeled. Played bridge all day.

Jan 20, 1945 – ¾ can of coffee, 1 can of milk, ½ box of sugar, 2 oz chocolate, ¾ box raisins, ½ box of crackers. We had a musical show at the RC room.

Jan 21, 1945 (Sunday) went to church and then played bridge. Nothing new.

Church, unfortunately, was not a highly organized affair at Stalag IV. The number one problem was that there was no chapel per se. The Red Cross distribution room was the only facility in which the men could gather for any event – such as the musical show he had attended on the 20th. It was not large enough to accommodate all the prisoners wishing to attend worship services – so they took turns – or it gave some the handy excuse not to go at all. There were three chaplains among the prisoners: Capt. Rev. T. J. B. Lynch, Catholic; a civilian internee, Rev. A. Jackson, protestant; and Capt. Rev. G. R. Morgan, Church of England. In setting up Stalag Luft IV, the Germans deprived the prisoners of anything religious they had possessed previously. In this regard, Rev. Jackson complained of the confiscation of Bibles, religious books and church furnishings – but to no avail. The activity of all three chaplains was greatly hampered by the fact that they could only go from one part of the camp to another accompanied by sentries – and these were often not available.

Lindsay writes occasionally about playing bridge and poker (at which he proved to be quite good), but this was done in the cramped quarters of the 20-feet-by-20 barracks room – occupied at times by a maximum of 24 men. There was a sports field within the camp, but no equipment was provided and there was no organized recreation – not even one soccer ball. In short, the Germans provided nothing to alleviate the boredom of incarceration. There was no theater and no canteen – and no facilities for individual preparation of Red Cross Food. That is why Sergeant Lindsay was elated on the few occasions when the mess hall provided "hot water". That was the only way to make use of the coffee and hot chocolate rations from the Red Cross.

But even that bit of consideration was coming to an end. The Red Army was moving relentlessly out of Russia and onto the plains of Poland. With the utmost urgency, the Soviet commander, General Georgy Zhukov, thrust his forces powerfully toward the German heartland. He had under his command 163 fighting divisions, 6,500 tanks, 32,000 artillery pieces, and 4,700 aircraft. War materiel, on the other hand, was dwindling rapidly for the Germans. They were being pressed on every side – from the east and west and south. On January 28 the Ardennes salient – the final bastion of strength on foreign soil for the Germans - was at last eradicated and the Allied armies thrust out of Belgium, across Holland, and into the Rhineland.

At this point, all that was happening externally caused a great deal of turmoil in the camp, and some prisoners were transferred – leaving only about 8,000. For more than a week Sergeant Lindsay failed to make a daily entry in his diary. He made up for it with a lengthy summary ten days later in which he gives special notation to "Big Stoop". This was Feldwebel Schmidt, who was also known by the prisoners as "Slap Ears" and "Ham Hands". He stood 6' 7", was heavyset with large hands, fair hair, and mean face and was just oafish. He was doubtlessly the most hated guard at Stalag IV – a triggerman for Fahnert. He physically abused hundreds of prisoners and pilfered supplies. (Lindsay's notation in his entry for the following day about "Big Stoop" served as a reminder for him, but gave no details for fear that his diary could be discovered and confiscated – in that event serious punishment could have ensued. This is one man to whom all the prisoners gave a wide berth.)

Jan 21, 1945 to Feb 2, 1945 – A period in which to remember "Big Stoop". A lot has really happened. Food has gotten to be a big problem. We have been cut to half (½) RC rations. It snowed almost (3) days in a row. Then it stopped, warmed up quite a lot – and then has been raining a lot. Bread rations from the Germans has stopped and that is really rough. Jan 1, 1945 "B" lager has been evacuated with the exception of a couple hundred and they moved into this lager.

Feb 2, 1945 – evacuated POWs moved to "B" lager. The eastern war is sure moving this way fast. Hope the Russians get here soon. Some of our wounded fellows from this lager have already left. It's really a pitiful sight to see these soldiers that have to move here on foot.

Feb 3, 1945 – Barley cereal for breakfast to take the place of the bread we don't get. Roll call – the ground is sure wet. The wounded soldiers (English, French, Russians, Poles, and just about every other soldier in Europe) come and go, their feet are swollen and blistered. Some have pneumonia. They are all just about starved. Most of them have been on the road for 15 days or more.

Feb 4, 1945 – They come and go – How long will it be before we leave, that's the $64.00 question?

(Most people in the 21ˢᵗ Century have no understanding of his last comment. The big game show on radio in the 1940s was "The $64 Question". During the program contestants would agonize over risking a secure $32, in order to go for the big prize. Whenever someone was brave enough to face a final question, the audience would respond in derision, "You'll be sorrrrry!")

Sergeant Lindsay explained years later that previous to the official declaration to abandon Stalag IV, rumors ran rampant among the prisoners. Under the uncertain conditions and with no definite word, the men surrendered their rationality to wild conjecture. Some predicted a mass desertion by the Germans, abandoning the *Kriegies* to fend for themselves until the Russians could liberate them – or they might be forced to fight their would-be liberators; or possibly be backed to the wall and mowed down like just so much grass. (*Kriegesgefangenen* was the German word for Prisoner of War. GIs, as they did with everything else, shortened it to call themselves *Kriegies*.) At any rate, the men could only guess as to what would happen next, as the frenzied guards and leaders scurried mysteriously around the camp. The suspense was finally relieved when the men were told that the order for evacuation of the camp had been received. The time designated was eight o'clock on the morning of February 5ᵗʰ. This news started an orgy of preparation for both the prisoners and the guards.

Each prisoner hastily arranged what little "stuff" he had for the trip – eating as much as possible of hoarded food so as to lighten the load.

Some expected a march of a month or two at the most, while others predicted a short jaunt of a few days. The Germans frantically organized schedules for the marching formations of all those physically able to move. Only the hospital cases, along with a few aides were being left behind. They were left with no provisions and only the most meager rations.

Once the Russians arrived there was no further word of them.

February fifth dawned, cold, wet, and gray. Stepping out of the loathsome wooden huts for the last time, prisoners were torn between elation at leaving the discomforts of the camp and uncertainty of the prospects of hardships yet to be endured on The March. No one could even imagine the misery that lay ahead.

Feb 5, 1945 – About 22:00 "Troy" came around to the Bks with the announcement we were moving at 10:00 the next morning. Everyone is eating like mad.

The war was going from bad to worse for the Germans, but they still had in mind the insidious plan to use Prisoners of War as a human shield, against the approaching war machine of the Allies. (Little did the Germans realize that such a plan would not be a problem for, nor delay the Soviet Red Army – they would uncaringly march through such a frail mass of humanity.) Camps all over the Eastern Front were evacuated and the prisoners pushed westward. Lindsay mentioned on February 2 that some of the wounded had left already – and not in transportation but on foot. Not many of them would last.

It became quite apparent that the end of the war was drawing nearer. Artillery fire and exploding bombs could be heard continuously night and day. For weeks the men had carefully hoarded some of their Red Cross food items, but with news on February 5 that they were to march out the next morning they ate as much as they could, since it would be difficult to carry it with them.

Most Americans are aware, at least in a general way, about the Bataan Death March that took place in the Philippines during April 1942. On April 9, American Major General Edward King, with food and medicine exhausted, surrendered a force of 11,000 American and 65,000 Filipino soldiers to the Japanese. In a forced march of 60 miles in tropical heat and without food and water, only 54,000 reached the destination of prison Camp O'Donnell. Mercilessly 22,000 died along the way due to heat prostration, starvation, dehydration, and disease and outright murder. Countless beheadings, slit throats, bayoneting, and other gruesome murders were rampant during the six bloody days of that march. News of the atrocities aroused great outrage across the United States. The Japanese became a hated enemy.

Unfortunately, a far more grueling March has been neglected by recorded history. Coming as it did at the end of the war, its gruesome details were lost in the euphoria of victory over the Nazi regime. It was during the winter and spring of 1945 that 8,000 American Air Force noncoms endured "The Black March". When they set out from Stalag IV it was in the midst of one of the most severe winters Europe had suffered in many years. (The only significant difference between the two merciless marches was the temperature – unbearably hot and humid on Bataan – below freezing, with ice and snow in Germany.) For 87 days the men marched westward along a meandering route of 600 miles. It proved to be a time of mass heroism, as the men aided one another in their difficult stumble forward. Fortunately, James B. Lindsay maintained his daily diary. This is the only written record of the stalwart manner in which the airmen managed their survival.

Chapter Six

THE START OF THE INFAMOUS BLACK MARCH

O n February 6, 1945, Soviet Red Army Forces of the 1st Ukrainian Front broke through the German defenses and across the Oder River, southeast of Breslau, Poland. No longer was there a recognizable Eastern Front – the battlefield was fluid from hour-to-hour. Instantly hundreds of thousands of panicked German civilians began to flee westward toward Dresden. Six years earlier, those same greedy Germans had boldly followed their conquering army into Poland. By brutal and often deadly force they pushed Polish farmers out of their homes, seizing possession of the land. From the bounty of the land they had reaped rich harvests. Now the circumstances had suddenly reversed and they fled in deadly fear of reprisals at the hands of the Russians and the Poles. The men of the once proud and mighty *Wehrmacht* (literally Defense Force) were not far behind. In cowardly fashion they foolishly discarded their weapons as they scurried away, yearning for the safety of the Fatherland. The roads were clogged with every kind of military and civilian contrivance, and consequently progress was slow. But as many struggled along on foot through the mud and snow the weather became a merciless foe - thousands fell victim to its icy grip.

Further to the west, Colonel Bombach was even more stern and brutal than usual as he oversaw the hasty evacuation of Stalag IV. He was tormented that his little kingdom was being eliminated. With just the one-day alert and little time to prepare themselves, more than 8,000 U. S. and a few British airmen began a forced march out of the prison camp toward the west - in below freezing temperatures. It was the coldest winter in Europe in all of the Twentieth Century. Angry guards with fixed bayonets used the butts of their rifles to shove slow moving men into line. They were angry and agitated because they too were being required to leave the relative comfort of their barracks and go out into the bleak and frozen weather. For what would prove to be inhuman and grueling conditions, the prisoners were provided with neither adequate clothing nor footwear. In fact, what they had had not been sufficient to keep warm in the bleak barracks. Now, in the open countryside, they shivered day and night – there was an inward chill in every man.

It took only a matter of hours for the horrible conditions of the barbed-wire prison camp to be left behind – only to be exchanged for the far worse experiences that lay ahead on what would come to be called "The Black March". Though this epic march was lost in the shuffle of all the chaotic events that took place in the closing months of the War, it nonetheless shows the stamina of brave prisoners in a horrific situation. Fortunately, Sergeant Lindsay left a detailed diary account of those three months that were frozen in the archives of history. In spite of every other burden he had to bear, he kept the thin 5 by 7 light brown notebook safe and dry.

Regardless of circumstances, or military emergencies, no human being should be forced to face the shockingly brutal conditions of such a March. There was a total lack of sanitary facilities – men could only relieve themselves in the open – not even necessarily at the side of the road. They left behind a dark trail of defilement. Worse than that, however, was a completely inadequate, starvation diet. When figured out later, it amounted to only about 700 calories per day per man. That was in stark contrast to the 3,500 provided by the U. S. military services. Malnourishment loomed large and certain along the entire length of the March. Red Cross food parcels provided some additional calories – but only when and if the Germans decided to distribute them (while pilfering from them for themselves).

As a result of the unsanitary conditions and a total lack of nutrition, disease became rampant: typhus fever was spread rapidly by body lice; dysentery was suffered in some degree by everyone; pneumonia, diphtheria, pellagra, and other diseases were nearly as deadly as the

German guards. A major problem, because of being constantly out in the open, was frostbite that in many cases resulted in the amputation of extremities – done in open field surgery with no anesthetic. At night the men slept on the frozen ground or, where available, in barns or any other shelter that could be found. With such large numbers, however, there was never space under a roof for everyone. But more of that later. Let Sergeant Lindsay put it in his own words.

Feb 6, 1945 – Barley cereal for breakfast for the last time at Stalag #4. We left at 10:00 and as we marched through the A lager we got a Red Cross food parcel. We are carrying what we can on our backs – food. Clothes and blanket roll. We are spending tonight in a large barn. These Germans stack men in a place like "sardines".

It was a rag-tailed, motley crew indeed that started out that day. Many of the *Kriegies* were wearing two or three complete outfits of pants, shirts and sweaters – everything they had accumulated. They also carried several extra food parcels, which had been hoarded for an emergency – or most recently stolen from the Red Cross warehouse.

At the onset of the March – in spite of the extremely foul weather – the prisoners rejoiced in the mere freedom of movement after so many long months of being confined in a compound devoid of physical activity. The boredom of incarceration had reduced most of the men to the attitude of doing nothing more strenuous than that required in attending to daily needs. Consequently, in a matter of a couple of days on the March, muscles that had been unused for long periods, collapsed under the strain of marching in the cold, wet weather of the Polish and German winter. Their bones and joints ached mercilessly and all the prisoners were seized with fierce attacks of cramps. When a halt was called - and tired, pain-wracked bodies were finally allowed to rest - it was difficult to get their legs in motion when it was time to move again. The men's distress was increased by the numbness and swelling of frostbite. And, due to the lack of sanitation facilities, the ever-present lice* that infested every man, introduced typhus. Dysentery marched along with them to add more misery to what was already unbearable. Some were unfortunate to be plagued with all the problems simultaneously – men who struggled to keep up the pace with bodies weakened by the fevers of typhus, the bodily disorders of dysentery, the pains of frostbite, persistent cramps due to exposure to the elements, and complete fatigue. It was a fight uphill in what seemed like a stiff wind all the way.

The five Allied doctors on the March were provided almost no medicines or help by the Germans. Those doctors, and a British chaplain, stood high in the ranks of the many heroes of the March. After walking all day, with frequent pauses to care for stragglers, they spent the night caring for the ill, and then marched again the next day. When no medication was available, their encouragement and good humor helped many a man who was on the verge of giving up.

*There are three kinds of lice that live on humans, and the *Kriegies* experienced all of them:

1. Head lice are usually found in the hair, most often at the back of the neck and behind the ears.

2. Public lice – also causes crabs.

3. Body lice – nets – live and lay eggs in the seams of clothing. They transfer to the body to feed.

Lice spread easily from one person to another through casual contact or shared items. A louse cannot jump or fly.

Feb 7, 1945 – up at 0600 – we did get hot water to make coffee. The Germans promised at least one hot meal a day. The packs are heavy and the fellows are throwing a lot of things away. We march about 1-½ hours and rest for about 5 mins. We got ½ hr for dinner – march, march, and march – to make things worse there is ice, snow, and mud. Then barns again – we stopped at Stolganberg this time.

Feb 8, 1945 – the same as yesterday. The march has really begun to tell. A few pass out along the way.

Acts of heroism were universal among the American and British prisoners – the stronger helped the weaker. Sometimes the Germans commandeered farm wagons when it became evident that some men were totally unable to walk. But seldom were there horses available, so teams of POWs struggled to pull the wagons along the rough roadways

– slipping and sliding through the snow. A mile or two of such exertion was about the maximum any *Kriegie* could expend – then others would take over. It was a pathetic sight – yet a valiant one as men struggled forward, determined not to be left behind. Occasionally stragglers fell along the roadside, unable to keep up the pace. They were never seen again. The five Allied doctors did what they could in an impossible situation. The most excruciating experience for them was to perform amputations under such conditions as if on a battlefield – with no anesthesia for the amputee. Captain Sommers, the German's chief medical officer, throughout the sickening three-month ordeal refused to give any aid to the sick or wounded on the March. His disdain for weakened and weary prisoners became the assumed attitude of the rank-and-file guards as well. There was never a hint of pity or compassion.

Feb 9, 1945 – We got about five potatoes from the farm – our first meal. A day of <u>rest</u> and most of the fellows certainly need it.

Feb 10, 1945 – We left this place about 7:00. Got my food back from the ox cart minus the blanket roll.

Feb 11, 1945 – Still marching – food from RC parcel getting low – no hot meal – Goes with the rest of the Germans words & promises – found a blanket.

Feb 12, 1945 – Still marching – two small blisters (not bad). A hot meal – about ½ pint of barley cereal.

In the beginning, a day's travel averaged seventeen kilometers. The Germans, however, considered that pace too leisurely and soon stepped it up to twenty and sometimes twenty-five kilometers a day. When the quota in miles had been reached, the prisoners were herded into deserted, rat infested barns and left to "lick their wounds". There was little or no shelter from the freezing cold and wind, since many of those buildings were lacking a wall or roof. When barns or similar structures were unavailable, the nights were spent where the men dropped – in ditches, fields, and forests. After a night spent on the cold, hard ground with no protection whatsoever, the comparative warmth of some ramshackle hut was welcomed.

Before dropping off to sleep, men prayed for strength to hold on just a little while longer, since each sunrise brought new hope. All physical and spiritual resources were mustered at the start of a day's march – and a little determined spring could be detected in the step of the men. But, pathetically such stamina soon faded. By nightfall the lines were once again reduced to straggling wisps of crawling men, begging only for a place to rest.

Feb 13, 1945 – A day of rest – such as it is – everyone is cold and hungry. Dewitt traded Lock's GI shoes for a loaf and a half of oat bran bread. Rec'd ¼ loaf of German rations.

Feb 14, 1945 – "St Valentines Day" and a day I am going to remember, started marching about 0700. About 14:30 we got a ½ milk can full of barley cereal and had to eat it while we marched along. It came from the field kitchen parked along the road. Been raining most of the day. At the usual stopping time we kept on marching and marched until after dark (about 8:00). The Germans stopped us in a cut of timber place and we spent the night in the open. It rained most of the night. What few things we have left are soaking wet. No food. This place is about 6 kms outside of Savinmunde. No hot water. Dewitt, Lockeny and myself drank a small amount of water from a ditch. Sure was thirsty.

It could only be by extreme necessity that Jim Lindsay would have ever stooped to such a low human condition – even as an adventurous kid and leader of the pack of boys back in Indiana. But conditions on the March seemed as if they were on a different planet. To be driven to such a point of exhaustion and thirst to drink water from a ditch shows what a desperate situation the prisoners were in. Because roadside water was often contaminated – even with human and animal excrement – dysentery and diarrhea were endemic among the men of the March. Complications of such illness, coupled with the fact that the average POW by this time had lost 1/3 of his body weight since capture, left the men as skeletal images of who they had been – Sergeant Lindsay was down to about 120 pounds.

A desire to once again eat his mother's strawberry shortcake – though admittedly the image was often dim - kept him going. Certainly he was determined not to be a straggler and fall behind. Often he heard the agonized groan of such men as they were bayoneted at the rear of the column – the Germans often not wasting a bullet on prisoners who were too weak to resist anyway. More compassionately, when a POW fell out along the road, a German guard would drop back and a shot would be heard. The guard would then come back into formation alone. No one was ever left behind alive.

Somehow the men continued to plod forward, averaging 15-20 miles per day. There was much zigzagging to escape the encroaching Soviet army from the east – the guards especially were anxious not to fall into the hands of the hated communists. Because of this, one day the *Kriegies* were pushed steadily for 40 miles, but in reality – because of circling back – they had advanced only a few miles to the west.

Feb 15, 1945 – marched to the docks at Swinemunde and caught a ferry to an island – walked about 25 km. No food – no hot water.

Feb 16, 1945 – still marching across the island – it seems to be a large island.

Feb 17, 1945. Got off the island – no food for 3 days – everyone is hungry. Stayed in a barn.

The incompetence of the Germans on the March was unbelievable. They had 8,000 men under their control - their responsibility – yet they did not offer them a scrap of food for three straight days. Nor was this the only time of such depravation – Sergeant Lindsay's diary lists many days in which the Germans gave the prisoners nothing to eat. Such cruelty – failing to provide a basic necessity of life - is unconscionable!

At this point it was only two weeks into the March. Prisoners had learned not to trust the Germans to provide anything good; but to have nothing at all hounded the road weary marchers. Even those who in the beginning had supplied themselves with extra rations felt the gnawing pains of starvation soon after their last precious morsel was eaten. The once strong bodies of these men - already ravaged outwardly by all the scourges of the March - were now also being attacked from within by this most insidious of enemies - no food - starvation. Having nothing to eat gnawed at their minds as well as their stomachs. The sight of the relatively well-fed guards drove many to a frenzy of frustration. When they had had the fortification of at least a little bit of food, the prisoners somehow found the strength to endure a day's march. But with nothing to eat - everything seemed impossible and the end was not in sight - too far away and too indefinite to compensate for the struggle and misery entailed in achieving it.

With no prospect of receiving food from the German guards, the men were forced to try to find food wherever and however they could. Occasionally they encountered someone with whom a trade could be negotiated. More than likely, this someone was a slave laborer, who was actually hardly better off than a prisoner. Even so, some had access to food, and after all language difficulties were overcome, a trade was made. With no money or anything else of value for barter, these deals were made in an exchange of food for cigarettes, which many foresighted *Kriegies* had hoarded for just such an eventuality. The amount of food procured in this manner was inconsequential; it could never be stretched far, and only served to whet the appetite, not satisfy it. Other sources of food had to be found. Prisoners dug in the fields where they walked, hoping to find a forgotten root or two left from the previous harvest. Only too often, a prisoner received nothing but cracked and bleeding hands after hours of digging in the frozen ground. Forests were stripped bare in the hunt for acorns and berries. In desperation, many *Kriegies* ate even the bark and leaves of trees. Here was man lowered to the level of animals, human scavengers, fighting for the chance to eat and to live that they might be men again - asking only for perseverance to live through the terrors of this March. The morale of the marchers had scraped the bottom. The shining lights of faith and hope were growing dim.

Feb 18, 1945 – marched – slept in an old barn. I am getting madder each day.

Feb 19, 1945 – left this barn about 1500, marched about 6 kms to another barn. We got 1/10 loaf bread, 1/10 can of German c beef and some plain lard. 1 milk can of lard sure was a treat.

Under normal circumstances most men would think of "lard" as "yuk". But under those conditions, the added fat content of the lard made it palatable.

Feb 20, 1945 – A day's rest - If that's what you call it. Got hot spuds twice.

Feb 21, 1945 – We got 1/3 R. C. parcel – Dewitt, Lockenny and myself. We were only supposed to have marched 12-14 kms but this turned out to be our hardest march – second only to that St. Valentine march. – Coming to the barn, the German Sgt. took us through swamps, plowed ground, over ditches and grassy mulch that came over the tops of our shoes. The German lady here seems to be pretty nice.

Feb 22, 1945 – A day of rest. Cooked a stew of potatoes, cabbages and onions. Traded for some potatoes, jam and bread. R. C. is OK – no bread or food from the Germans – just promises.

Living under such a threat of starvation, prisoners bartered with German civilians whenever possible. Using cigarettes, watches, rings or whatever they had of value, they traded with farmers along the way for food. In doing so, however, they risked the lives of both themselves and the farmers. Colonel Bombach gave strict orders to his henchmen that there was to be no fraternization with the enemy – he knew that in a weakened condition the prisoners were less of a threat to his authority – such thinking was a fit for his sadistic mentality. Even so it was no easy task to control less than 8,000 men (the number was decreasing daily), who - when stretched out for a day's march - were at least two miles from front to back. Each day, when the first men began to walk, it was another half-an-hour before the end of the column fell into line. The Germans were frantic in their effort to keep the prisoners under control, and the denial of food – even if they had had it to give – was a powerful weapon of choice.

But a lack of food was not the only problem facing the prisoners.

The long column of men was a weary waste of pain, infection, and contamination. What food they did consume passed through them rapidly because of dysentery and diarrhea. To stave off the ravages of such disease, the men ate charcoal when they could find it – but it was not very effective. The only growing, living thing among them was lice – every POW was infected. Along with the little varmints - pneumonia, pellagra, typhus, trench foot, tuberculosis and other diseases ran rampant among the weary men of The Black March.

The numbing cold was an added misery that spared no one – including the guards. One would have to experience the damp air of a German winter to understand what these men endured. It was a penetrating type of cold air that seeped all the way into the bone – and seemed to freeze there. As they trudged forward day-after-day, each man was convinced in his own mind that he could never be warm again. It was a despicable, dispiriting sensation, which often caused shivers to run down the spine - shivers that seemed would never stop. Even so, there was compassion within the ranks – if a man had an extra sweater or coat he would pass it on to a prisoner who only had rags left for clothing. On the surface such an act seems insignificant, but considering the uncertainty of the situation – when not knowing how the misery would end - each such gesture was a true expression of heroism and sacrifice.

Feb 23, 1945 – Started out and got about 5 or 6 kms and then stopped for 2 hrs and turned around and came back to the same barn. It rained on the way back. Still no food from the Germans.

Feb 24, 1945 – Still here at the barn. We have R.C. rations of 1 can pate, 3 lumps of sugar and a little milk left – no food from Germans. The German lady gave us hot water and spuds.

Feb 25, 1945 – What the fellows are eating they trade cigarettes, rings, clothes and watches for. We got some potato soup from the German lady. Most of the fellows are cold and hungry and a lot of them are sick. G. I.s

Feb 26, 1945 – Started out again and got 3 or 4 kms then turned around again. Received 2/5 loaf of bread, 3/5 lb butter. We got some hot spuds and pickled pork fat. It has been doing a lot of raining. We got our blankets wet this morning.

Feb 27, 1945 – This morning the sun was out for a little while. Had a pate sandwich for breakfast with coffee – that is finish for R. C. rations. Dewitt is feeling better. He has been sick for the past ten days. G. I.s Had some good potatoes and carrot soup. No bread ration. Our back bread ration is almost finished. Dewitt traded for some Jerry jam.

Feb 28, 1945 – Last night I fell off of the hay pile. It didn't hurt me, but Lockenny thought it was funny. What a way to wake up. Ha'Ha. We got some hot water this morning for hot coffee. Lock and I got some hot water and shaved. This afternoon the sun was out and we got around in the sun. Got some potato soup about 1600. Lockenny and Dewitt are out of cigarettes. Our bread is also gone.

It is so inspirational to read of how these men maintained their dignity in spite of the extreme depravation they experienced. "Shaving" is a manly activity, which gives a sense of newness and reinvigoration – especially with the tingle of a splash of after-shave lotion. But in this case, shaving was obviously still a pleasure worth mentioning – even if accomplished by using hot water in a bowl.

Lindsay's last sentence is difficult for most people even to imagine. It is a mournful thought. What does it do to a man's sense of hope – if he has no bread?

Chapter Seven
MARCHING ON THROUGH MARCH

It was an incredible, almost impossible, experience for the American and British Prisoners of War to get up and go day-after-day, forced to march in a slipshod manner across the frozen north central part of Germany. If there had been some hope or evidence of reward in return for their effort it would have been different, but there was nothing – just a meaningless daily grind. It also became increasingly difficult to gauge the attitude of the guards. Some of them seemed to be even more surly and cruel with each passing day. They were watching the destruction of their country and considered the airmen of the United States as the primary culprits. This was especially true of "Big Stoop" (Feldwebel Schmidt). He openly and wantonly brutalized prisoners without provocation and continued to steal from what little was left from the dwindling precious Red Cross parcels. It was well known to everyone that he was the obedient right hand man for Oberfeldweble Fahrnert and was delighted to follow through on every command of the Captain. Or even worse, he freely exercised his authority without direct orders from above. So whenever men saw his big frame approaching they instinctively turned away, hoping not to draw his attention.

Especially frustrating to the airmen was the fact that it was obvious the Germans had no idea of what they were doing – other than keeping out of reach of the massive Soviet army that was steamrolling westward. On the particular day when they trudged steadily for ten hours, covered forty miles, and wound up circling back to approximately where they had started, the POWs were more angry than tired. None of it made any sense. But such a meandering passage was not unusual. For that matter, because of the heavy war damage, the inadequacy of the roads, and the fluidity of the flow of battle, not all the POWs even followed the same route to the west. This was a great frustration to Commandant Bombach because he could not really control the situation to his satisfaction. He was also bothered deeply by what he observed to be the increasingly relaxed attitude of a few of the men under him - those who were not ardent Nazis. As the sound of Allied artillery grew closer and knowing that the end was near, some guards were less harsh in their treatment of the prisoners - surely hoping for leniency when the tables were turned. Even so the *Kriegies* knew better than to put any trust in any of their tormentors.

March 1, 1945 – Hot water – 1 R.C. parcel per man also 1/3 loaf of bread and ¼ lb of butter. It began raining and the wind is really blowing. The doctor had us move to another barn and what a mess.

March 2, 1945 – Hot water for coffee. We moved out at 0800 – muddy as anything. Marched about 25 kms and stayed in a barn near the town of Waren. The doctor took our beds again and made us all mad Lockenny included.

These airmen had been conditioned from their first days in basic training to obey orders – and in the service of their country they were pleased to do so because most orders made sense. But it was extremely frustrating to have to obey orders from the "supposed doctor" of the Germans – Captain Sommers. Not only was he unsympathetic to the prisoners' suffering, but also he did every little thing he could to make matters worse. Of what benefit was it to him to take away their beds? There was no medical reasoning behind it - just another means of adding misery to what was already unbearable.

For that matter, "beds" is a misnomer. By it, Sergeant Lindsay is referring to the simple comfort of a blanket. Other than that, the only "bed" he had for the three months on the long March was a bit of hay or the hard ground. In fact, the "bed" was a rolled up blanket – or two - that each man carried along each day. During the course of the March these naturally became ragged, dirty, often wet, infected with vermin, and unfit for human use. Nonetheless, it was their only bit of comfort in a totally hostile situation. No wonder Lockenny was mad. Why should he, or anyone, be deprived of this one small token of coziness?

The scars of sickness, starvation and despondency could be detected in the thinning lines of those who staggered forward. Each day, an untold number were left behind. Those were men whose will to live had been squelched under the duress of endless, intolerable misery – men who once had been full of energy, but now were drained of the last dregs of human endurance. A few attempted escape on the assumption that nothing could be worse than the tortures of that walking death, but none got very far since they had no resources. During the three arduous months of the March, an estimated 1300 *Kriegies* didn't make it. Left behind in barns and along the way, they were those who could no longer crawl or drag their weakened bodies into the lines. They pleaded piteously to be carried until some strength could be regained, but as time dragged on few men could muster enough energy to bear the extra burden and these pleas had to be ignored. Some of the men left behind caught up in the last days of the March, but the whereabouts of many will never be known and it is impossible to speculate as to their fate.

Days lost their identity as the meaninglessness of the March was repeated over and over. The weeks crept by in endless monotony. What were petty gripes at first became serious complaints. Two long months had already been spent just marching, marching. Every man wanted to rebel but could not since there was no alternative - and the result was an attitude of dejected resignation. The men doggedly plodded along in the completely mechanical routine of putting one foot in front of another through all the hours of daylight - then getting what little rest could be found in the few fitful hours of the night.

March 3, 1945 – Got potatoes and hot water – ate the last of the raisins. The wind made walking more miserable than ever. Passed through Waren. All the roads are still crowded with refugees moving ahead of the Russians. Dead horses are all along the road. Stopped at a barn about 6 kms from Malchon.

March 4, 1945 – Got hot water (very lucky because a lot of the fellows didn't), rec, 1/5 loaf of bread, 1/5 lb butter and a very small amount of meat. Also we got some meat broth and potatoes. During the march the snow fell quite hard and it was driven by a hard wind. We marched approx 20 kms.

March 5, 1945 – Got hot water – R. C. is running short. Passed through Karshon. Lockenny is really mad at the Germans today. We were on muddy roads and his feet were giving him trouble. We three (Lockenny and Dewitt) were lucky to have bed space. A lot of the fellows had to sit up. The name of the town is Weisin.

March 6, 1945 – Got 1/10 loaf of bread. The sun was out all day. Only marched 11 kms. Got here in the barn at noon. Hot water and potato soup.

March 7, 1945 – A day of rest. Got both hot water and barley cereal. Bread is all gone. Potato soup at noon and 5 spuds for supper. The Germans gave us 2/5 loaf of bread, 1/5 lb butter. A jet plane flew over in the afternoon.

March 8, 1945 – Hot water – soup – spuds. The weather was bad the entire day (misty snow). Another (jet plane) flew over. We remained here at the same barn as yesterday.

Although Lindsay had been a prisoner for only four months, the warring parties in the global conflict continued to maximize their efforts. The jet he saw high in the sky had been talked about for years. Now it had become a reality and he was fascinated by its speed. In 1944 the German Luftwafe introduced into combat the first jet aircraft – the Messerschmitt ME 262. It was by far the fastest airplane in the war – at 541 mph it was a hundred-miles-an-hour faster than anything the Allies had at their disposal at that time. Such an air speed difference could have given the Germans a decisive advantage in aerial combat – if it had become a factor earlier. Fortunately for the Allies, however, its final development came too late to have a determining effect on the outcome of the conflict in the air. The consistency of the bombardment campaign by the Americans and British seriously hampered the German industrial efforts. Consequently, production of the jet had been distributed to many small factories, so that by the end of the war they had built only 1,400 of them.

American ingenuity, however, was not far behind and a far superior jet was about ready for combat. Meanwhile, on the ground the American push against the Nazis from the west reached into the heartland of Germany – advanced patrols of the U.S. First Army entered Cologne on March 5, 1945 and captured it the next day. Unfortunately, the once beautiful city had been reduced to rubble from incessant Allied bombing. At the same time the U. S. Third Army reached the Rhine Northwest of Koblenz, Cologne (Koln) fell completely to the U. S. First Army. The distance separating the prisoners on the March from the American and British forces was lessening with each passing day.

The war had so deteriorated for the Germans that they now began conscripting 15 and 16-year-olds into the regular army. This raised angry response from the public, which could read the handwriting on the wall. The war was lost – why waste the lives of more youth? But the military had its way – as always the German pride of country trumped all reason.

March 9, 1945 – Had tea for breakfast. Bread and R.C. all gone. Now we shall have to rely upon the Germans for food. This is a fine day just like spring. March approx 10 kms. Had 4 spuds and a cup of soup for supper. We all three have body lice.

March 10, 1945 – Marched approx 12 kms. The sun was warm but the wind was cold. Passed through Parchin around noon. We had potatoes – soup and potatoes – This seems to be our best ration since we started.

March 11, 1945 – A day of rest, Zeisbuger. Drank plain hot water for breakfast and had some hot potatoes for dinner. Dewitt traded for a loaf of bread (cigarettes). The spuds we got for dinner had to last us all day because the Germans fed the pigs the ones we were to have for supper. (Everybody is happy.)

March 12, 1945 – Had some warm spuds for breakfast. March 12-14 kms. We saw two p-51s about noon – they gave us a buzz job and really looked nice. 1/5 loaf of bread 2/9 lb butter from Jerry. (6 days) Dewitt got a cocoa can full of salt for two bars of soap and I got a milk can full of sugar the easy way – from a warehouse.

Sighting the P-51 Mustangs had to be an inspiration to Jim and the other prisoners, who could observe its potential from the ground. It was arguably the best aircraft of World War Two – if not all time. As a weapon and as an aircraft it was in every way superb. Compared to the ineffectual Messerschmitt ME 262 jet, (noted earlier) the P-51, on the average flew faster, further, and safer. The Mustang outperformed and outmatched everything it faced. The plane's mission of protecting American bomber fleets was fulfilled so completely that Luftwafe pilots did not dare to come close to it. In fact, by this time the Mustangs had destroyed almost all of Germany's single engine fighters.

March 13, 1945 – We reached the town of Dambeck around 1300 – from here we are supposed to get transportation (we shall see). Got nice potatoes for supper – there is close to a 1000 men in the barn.

March 14 1945 – Just hanging around. Spuds for breakfast, a milk can full of barley soup for supper. Around 1400 there was a great deal of bombing going on close by.

Indeed, as the airmen were waiting for transport – crowded as they were in a drafty barn – they listened daily to the Allied bombing campaign against nearby Hanover. Because it was such an important road junction and industrial center, the air attacks against it became increasingly intense. As a result of a total of 88 sorties, involving hundreds of aircraft, 90 percent of the city center was destroyed. Worse, however, in a design to hopefully shorten the war, residential areas were also specifically targeted – in which 6,000 residents were killed. This was not the result of what is referred to today as "collateral damage". On the contrary, it was a specific strategy designed to break the spirit of the citizens of the nation. Sergeant Lindsay's expression of sympathy for the people in his entry for the next day is amazing in the light of what he and his fellow prisoners were enduring.

March 15, 1945 – (Thursday) this is Lockenny's birthday. I gave him a pack of cigarettes and he was sure glad to get them. The boys were over again and one of them kicked a bomb out near by. It isn't anything though to hear bombs and guns in Germany. I don't see how the people stand it. (Hard luck)

By this time the air lanes were controlled almost totally by the Americans and British – Field Marshall Herman Goering's once proud Luftwafe was now smashed and ineffective. Yet the German ground forces continued to battle forcefully in the West. Even at this late date in the war neither Belgium nor the Netherlands had been cleared of the stubborn German occupational troops. Nonetheless, the push by the Allies continued on all fronts.

On March 17, 1945, the U. S. Third Army overran Koblenz. But tragedy also struck on that day. The Ludendorff Bridge at Remagen, seized by U.S. troops on the 7th of March, suddenly collapsed, killing dozens of U. S. Army engineers who were working to reinforce it.

From his bunker in Berlin, Adolph Hitler grew increasingly fearful of what he saw as the inevitable victory of the Allied Forces. In a frantic move, bordering on hysteria, he ordered the demolition of all German industrial, utility and transport facilities deemed to be in danger of falling into enemy hands. Armaments minister Albert Speer was ordered to carry out the insane instructions. For years he had been a loyal devotee of Hitler, and was the master production planner of Germany's war effort. Nonetheless, in this case he sabotaged the order, which in German is Verbrannte Erde – Scorched Earth. This was the only time he ever disobeyed the Fuhrer. In like manner, most local commanders also did not follow through on the order. Realizing that the war would soon be lost, they knew that such destruction would be a devastating loss to the general population. It seems that Sergeant Lindsay understood and appreciated the plight of the people far better than their Fuhrer did.

Mar 16, 1945 – Friday – spuds and soup. Lock's tail gunner, Rendall had to go to the hospital. The sun was in and out all day.

Mar 17, 1945 – It is cloudy and rainy so we three are spending the day in bed.

Mar 18, 1945 – Sunday – The promised bread ration did not come in. We got 1/5 R. C. parcel and 1/5 lb Jerry marg. We ate most of ours as fast as we could divide it.

Mar 19, 1945 – Left around 9:30. Marched about 20 kms. Stayed in a hayloft with 150 men. Our cooks put out more spuds than we have ever had. I went in the back door of a house and picked up a pocketful of onions. Beautiful day.

German civilians had no idea what to do with the ragged, filthy Americans. In a few cases they provided what little they could in bartering/exchange with the Kriegies. But most of the time, fearing the worst, they shunned them. Hungry and searching for any scrap of food, the POWs would wander through any unlocked door and "borrow" whatever they could find.

March 20, 1945 – Tuesday – Marched about 20 kms – windy – We got about 10 nice potatoes for supper. R. C. is all gone.

March 21, 1945 – Crossed the Elbe River. Marched 18-20 kms. It was a pretty nice day.

Mar 22, 1945 – Marched approx 18 kms – weather was really wonderful. We got about 10 nice potatoes.

Mar 23, 1945 – A day of rest. I washed the socks for the three of us. Dewitt and Lock washed their long johns. We all three washed our heads for the fist time and I shaved. Sun was out nice and hot – 1/5 loaf of bread.

Mar 24, 1945 – Marched 16 kms, weather nice. The guards seem to be getting a sport out of hitting the fellows with sticks and gun butts. Dewitt and Lock went after bread and missed out on half of the spuds. We rec 3/5 loaf bread, 1/5 lb butter to last 6 days. They also gave us some horsemeat, but wouldn't give us time to cook it. The guard fired his gun while trying to put us in the barn. It was dark and on the way to my bed I fell out of the hayloft. I was very lucky because I fell on a loaf of black bread I had in my jacket. It didn't hurt me or the bread.

Mar 25, 1945 – "Palm Sunday" marched about 14 kms. The guards are still hitting a few of the fellows. A very nice day, in fact too hot to be marching with this load and these heavy clothes. Nice spuds, Jerry tea. We are all sweating out P. C. Parcels.

Mar 26, 1945 – A day of rest at the town of Barnm. Jerry coffee for breakfast, spuds and turnip soup for dinner, spuds for supper. This is the first time with L. J. Edwards group and he seems to do pretty good. We finished our bread and have about three days to do without unless we trade for some.

Mar 27, 1945 – the cooks got some Jerry coffee from the German lady. Dewitt traded his wedding ring off for a loaf of hot bread. Lock and I told him he was crazy and then thanked him and we had a chunk of bread. (Thanks Norm) Spuds for dinner and soup for supper.

March 28, 1945 – Jerry tea and the two rations of spuds. Lockenny and Dewitt went on a soup detail and ate all they wanted and brought me back more than I could eat. Thanks fellows. We are expecting to catch a train from here. The other barns have left. We got ready to move and they marched us ½ km to another barn. Then about an hour later they came and told us we had 2-½ hrs to march 12 kms and catch a train. We had to almost run, but we made the hike in 2 hrs flat. Dewitt and I were separated from Lock for the first time. Our car has 50 men. Lockenny got in a car with 100 men in it. The name of the town is Uelzen.

Mar 29, 1945 – We got ½ butter and 1/3 loaf of bread. There wasn't much sleep last night because you could hardly set up. We are eating raw spuds and rye, which we picked up at the last barn.

Mar 30, 1945 – We went through another "hellish" night. This morning we ate our last two thin slices of bread with a raw spud sliced on top to make a sandwich – not bad, but not enough. Arrived a Stalag XIA about 10:00 or 11:00. There are several different nationalities here. Coming into the camp we were searched. We sleep on the ground in large tents, which hold about 400 or 500 men. We had no food today.

From the start of the war the German government busied itself not only in fighting a determined enemy, but also in building at least a hundred internment camps. Many of them were used for slave labor, but six of them were for extermination purposes only – to murder and dispose of millions of Jews and other enemies of the state – such as the mentally impaired and physically crippled. As the war progressed, the Germans also had to construct more than fifty camps to accommodate nearly 300,000 American Prisoners of War. By the time Lindsay arrived at Stalag Luft IV, they had built more than 40 Stalag camps – short for Stammlager – for lower ranking regular Army soldiers. A half dozen, camps were designated Luft for airmen; and another seven Oflag camps for officers. There was need for only one Marlag prison - for navy personnel. Stalag XIA, at Altengrabow, Germany – at which Lindsay had a short stay - was one of the oldest, opened in November 1939. The March continued from there.

Mar 31, 1945 – Sat – last night was a most miserable one – cold and hungry and it rained. The ground was already wet and that ground was hard. I cooked up a can of rye this morning, which we were lucky to have. We had 1/3 of a can each. Our fighters had a nice dog fight right over our heads and the guards chased us into the tents. The promised soup from Jerry didn't come in so we have nothing to eat. Paules told us that the other Americans here are going to do without tomorrow so we can have something to eat.

What an ennobling sense of sharing this exhibited on the part of the permanent prisoners at Stalag XIA. They caught one glimpse of the bedraggled men of the Black March and decided to allocate what little they had to these who were obviously starving.

Meanwhile the war was going from bad to worse for the Germans as the full force of American participation reached its maximum. By 1945 a total of 16.1 million Americans had put on the uniform of the various services. In doing so, more than 405,000 gave their lives in the service of their country – 291,557 directly in combat. The impact of their sacrifice is inestimable in the destruction of the Nazi menace. Six years earlier the Germans had proudly stormed into Holland, conquerors of all who opposed them. Now they started pulling out. But perhaps even more disconcerting to the Nazi pride was when the French First Army crossed the Rhine for the first time since Napoleon in 1810. Also on this date the United States Third Army reached the city of Slegen – thirty miles east of the Rhine.

With rapid successes on the ground, the American First and Ninth Armies linked up at Lippstadt. In doing so they cut off 350,000 German troops in the Ruhr Valley area.

Could rescue be far away for the struggling men on the Black March? Or would Colonel Bombach keep them moving on his meaningless walk to nowhere? Yes! Beyond all understanding of anything intelligent or decent the March continued.

Chapter Eight
AGAINST ALL HOPE - HOPE

In reading Jim Lindsay's daily diary of the desperate days he spent as a Prisoner of War, one is struck by the almost total lack of anger toward his captors. It is evident in what he wrote that he had absolutely no degree of respect for the Germans. This was especially true during the long Black March when he and the other airmen were deprived of even a minimal supply of food, while forced to walk as much as forty miles in one day. Though he went down to as low as 120 pounds from his normal weight of 180, he somehow kept his spirit high. Perhaps this was because of his prediction from his first day at Stalag IV when he boldly told the others that he would be eating strawberry shortcake in Kokomo, Indiana, for his birthday in June. He never mentioned it again, but it must have been an internal goal that he intended to achieve. Hope, after all, is the internal spark of the human soul. Without it, even if not a Prisoner of War, that person will wither away. Unfortunately, that is what happened to hundreds of men on the March. Disease and fatigue and hunger were powerful enemies, which made it difficult to see beyond the horrible conditions of even a day. Since the past was terrible, and the present despicable, few men looked forward with expectancy

Beyond that toughness of the human spirit, perhaps Jim received solace from what he remembered of God's promise of life in the Scriptures through faith as he had learned as a teenager from Pastor Ruby. Though he didn't have a Bible of his own – occasionally borrowing one from someone else - he did a pretty good job of writing out from memory the prayer Jesus taught His disciples ("are" instead of "our daily bread"). He turned frequently to the back page of his diary to meditate on it:

<u>*The Lord's Prayer*</u>
St. <u>Matthew 6</u>
Our Father which art in heaven, Hallowed be thy name.
Thy kingdom come. Thy will be done in earth, as it is in heaven.
Give us this day are daily bread.
And forgive us our debts, as we forgive our debtors.
And lead us not into temptation, but deliver us from evil: for thine is the kingdom, and the power, and the glory, for ever. Amen

Now back to the diary itself.

April 1, 1945 – "Easter Sunday" – Well today I am thinking of both Lawrence & Paul (Happy Birthday Bud & Happy Easter Paul.) We three slept a little better last night. Dewitt & I got some moss and sticks and it makes a pretty good bed. Well we were so hungry that we were almost too weak to move & then God brought in 2 R.C. parcels for 11 men. We also got a can of soup and we feel pretty good again. Of course the R. C. is almost gone. We traded two pks of cigarettes for 1/3 loaf of bread and a can of Ovaltine. All this helped to fill up the big hole but we are still dreaming of food.

It's remarkable that in spite of the fact that he literally did not know where his next meal was coming from, he was able to keep his facts straight. This makes his diary all the more real and believable. The reason for his reflection on his two brothers on that particular day was that his brother Lawrence – also known as Bud, who was five years older – was born on April 1, 1919. His younger brother Paul had the middle name Easter because he was born on Easter Sunday, April 4, 1926. Though he had no way of knowing their circumstances, he assumed that both of them at that time were still serving stateside in the United States Army.

It is equally remarkable that such a small amount of food could "fill up the big hole". But of course, going for months without sufficient food, his stomach had shrunk considerably.

April 2, 1945 – Monday – the weather is really nasty. A lot of rain &
very windy. We are all so full of lice that it is pitiful but there isn't much
we can do about it. What we need is a good hot shower & some clean
clothes. We got a can of soup & Dewitt traded another pk of cig. for 4 sqs
of chocolate (very tasty).

The problem with lice was not something new for the prisoners.
Even when they were in the wooden barracks at Stalag IV there were no
facilities for bathing or delousing. Each barracks room there had only
one pan for washing hands, face, body, and (yuk) dishes. All water had
to be carried into the barracks from the pumps outside in the compound.
Consequently fleas, lice, scabies and bed bugs were everywhere. Since
the Germans furnished no insecticide or delousing powder, it was not
possible for the men to protect themselves from the infectious insects.
Now that they had been on the open road for more than two months,
the problem was even worse. No matter how much the men scratched
at them, the little varmints wouldn't go away – they too were hungry
– sucking the very life-blood of the Kriegies. It is amazing that under
such conditions there was no widespread outbreak of typhus.

April 3, 1945 – Tuesday. The R. A. F. hit this place last night. It seems
as though everyone likes to hear the sound of the planes and bombs ("KEEP-
EM-FLYING"). Dewitt & I went out after firewood and it had to rain so
we came back soaked. Well we are now on German rations again. 1/6 of
a loaf of bread, 1/25 lb of butter & a spoonful of jam. We also got a can
of soup.

"Keep-em- flying" became a repetitive theme for Jim Lindsay for
the rest of his life. He saw something both beautiful and vital in the
powerful beasts of war. He was struck with a deep sense of pride (even
while a prisoner) that he too was an airman – who saw an unmistakable
value in keeping them in the air.

April 4, 1945 – Wednesday – Well Paul you are the first one I thought
of this morning. 1/6 loaf of bread, 1/13 lb of butter. We rec. ½ R. C. #10

food parcel and one can of soup. Dewitt got 2 boxes of prunes & 2 D boxes for 4 ½ pks of cigarettes across the fence.

April 5, 1945 *Thursday – The R. A. F. bombing last night was too close for comfort. Dewitt as usual was shaking like a leaf in the breeze. For breakfast we had cereal (pre-mixed R.C.) with prunes added. We have only one roll call a day and it comes off at 8:00 each morning. We got our bread & butter, soup & brew from the Jerrys and ate like mad from our R. C. rations. Lock doesn't think my stomach could be filled with an entire cooked cow. I did get a little sick during the night though - Ha Ha.*

April 6, 1945 *Friday – We cooked a box of prunes after roll call. The morning hasn't been cold although it has been misty. We ate our bread ration all at one time with our "Jerry Brew". The Jerry coffee is plenty sweet. I sorta like it.*

April 7, 1945 *– We stayed in the sack until the last minute this morning then made roll call and hit the sack again. I spent the day reading from the "Bible". We had one slice of bread when the ration came in and then ate the other with a can of C rations at brew time.*

April 8, 1945 "Sunday". "Well thanks Lockeny for you know what." *Roll call – Jerry bread ration, butter, jam – good pan soup about 1300 & brew about 1800. The bombers can be seen or heard around this place day and night. We got a good rumor at bedtime and going to sleep with happy thoughts.*

April 9, 1945 *– "Monday" – 8:00 roll call. The weather is certainly nasty outside. Lock & I heated three cans of water – sold one & made two brews. The sun finally came out & we all shaved – then Dewitt & I washed a few clothes. Soup & Jerry brew. Paules told me today that we would get R. C. rations in the morning. I hope so. Ours was finished 2 days ago.*

The Paules he referred to was Frank Paules who was camp leader of Stalag Luft IV – and spokesman for the prisoners during The Black March. Although thousands of Allied airmen suffered at their hands, not much detail was left after the war about the Germans who ran this deplorable camp. Paules knew them well, having been at Stalag VI and experienced "the run up the road" (as detailed earlier). The personal narratives, which Paules gave after the war, are the most authoritative descriptions of these officers and their actions:

"Lt. Col. Bombach was about 38 years old, 5 ft. 6 inches tall. He had very thin features with black hair combed straight back. He was somewhat of a dandy, nervous fidgety type, and a Nazi Party man. I believe he was an espionage agent in France, speaks good English (but not openly) and understands English very well. He was in Command of Luft 4 and had been deputy Commandant of Luft 6 under Col Von Hoermann. Bomback was in charge of the camp and sanctioned and supported violations of the Geneva Convention.

"The Abwehr (security) officer was Capt. Lindemann, who was very weak and passive; not a forceful officer. Under him was Sgt. Fahnert, who actually ran the Abwehr activities in the camp. He was the power behind the throne, and he was present on the run up the road. The Germans, who beat the men, were under his orders at all times. It was reported to me that Fahnert had struck men on numerous occasions, and had kicked me. In spite of his rank he was on extremely intimate terms with both Captain Walter Pickhardt and Lt. Colonel Bombach. His authority in the camp was a great deal more than his rank would have called for. Within the camp he had a record of persecution and violence, and personally led all searches of the camp area. It was always believed by me that these three men – Bombach, Pickhardt and Fahnert were ardent Nazis. I was so informed on many occasions by friendly German personnel. The last thing I recall about Sgt. Fahnert was being threatened by him with shooting, for interfering with the distribution of Red Cross Parcels (on the occasion of leaving Stalag Luft IV to begin the march back to the western front).

"The rumor among the German personnel was that Lt. Col. Bombach was an espionage agent in France in 1940; and that in some fashion, Sgt. Farnert was also connected with him at that time. Fahnert always impressed me to either be a high member of the Nazi party or an undercover Gestapo agent (or hold some other high office or position). Since he had a great deal more authority than is generally given to Sergeants or other Non-Coms. It seemed almost as though Sgt. Fahnert, in matters of camp security, exerted a great deal of pressure on the camp commandant.

"Capt. Pickhardt was the captain of the guards, although they were not part of the Abwehr. On the run up the road, it was he who kept exhorting the German guards to use their bayonets; alongside the roadside, machine guns were set up in the woods and German soldiers were observed in the trees with cameras. Pickhardt kept yelling at the prisoners to escape, presumably to enhance a mass break, and subsequently give them a reason to kill us all. According to the testimony given to me by friendly German guards, Pickhardt had chosen men to supervise the run, whose homes had been bombed by the Allies. Many times, as prisoners were being counted by the guards inside the camp, he would strut up and down the ranks screaming: '*Schweinhunde*' and *Luftgansters*' (swine dogs and air gangsters).

"It was reported by friendly German personnel that during his many speeches to the guards, he stated it would be better if the POWs were all shot, then they would not have to feed them; that POWs were swine and not to be treated as men. He was always extremely abusive verbally. Pickhardt was one of the most fanatical Nazis I ever encountered in Germany. He had the complete confidence of the camp Commander, and the regime of terror seemed to be part of a plan carefully mapped out by both Bombach and Pichardt."

April 10, 1945 – *8:00 – roll call – Lock & I heated some water & had a good brew – 1/5 of a loaf of bread, 1/25 lb of butter & a small chunk of cheese. We ate the cheese and a little bread just before soup – barley soup & potatoes about 12:30. B-17s & B-24s blasted this place around 3 or 4. We saw 8 chutes from one plane. Jerry coffee & then to bed.*

April 11, 1945 – *8:00 roll call – 1/6 loaf of bread & 1/12 lb of butter. They ran out of soup and we didn't get it until brew came in – then they ran out of brew and we don't get ours until tomorrow. Dewitt, Lockenny & myself traded our jackets for British Battle Jackets. I hope to look back on these days of starvation soon and laugh. We spend most of our time lying around because we are all too weak to do much.*

April 12, 1945 – *Thursday – No roll call & a few minutes later Paules made the announcement that we were moving (We had heard the rumble and roar of artillery fire during the night. We got 2/5 of a Red Cross parcel and a few small items from Argentine bulk rations – 1 loaf of bread & ¾ lb butter. We left about 11:00 & marched till about midnight, approx 16 kms and slept in an open field.*

<u>April 13, 1945</u> - We had our morning coffee and Dewitt & I toasted some bread. We heard that our President died. Lock and I left our overcoats but Dewitt is carrying one of them. We marched about 17 kms and slept in a barn. It rained a little just before we got in the barn and we all three were sick during the night.

President Franklin Roosevelt died in mid-afternoon on April 12 after suffering a cerebral hemorrhage. The German guards were elated with the news, and gloated over his death and slandered his name with filthy language. They also berated the American airmen, bragging that now the war would turn in favor of Germany since the leader of the Allies was gone. It was but a dismal ray of hope for them. They were right, of course, in the sense that Roosevelt had been a strong force in the leadership of the Allies. Under his administration the United States arose from its prewar lethargy and had become "The Arsenal of Democracy". American industrial power exerted itself to provide the Allied military effort with most of the armaments needed to fight tyranny in every corner of the world. The American people rallied to the war struggle and the nation experienced a vast expansion of industry, which in turn wiped away the final remnants of The Great Depression.

Unknown to the general public, President Roosevelt had been in declining health for many years – even before the start of his presidency. His aides, who were certain that the American public would have greater confidence in a man of strength, had cleverly concealed this debilitation. But, in spite of his continual pain from the effects of infantile polio, he had the privilege of seeing the light at the end of the tunnel – the nightmare of war was drawing to a close. In Europe Germany was all but defeated and in the Far East Japan was being pushed back across the Pacific in a painstaking and deadly struggle – one island at a time. And, also dear to Roosevelt's heart, the formulation of the United Nations, which he had championed aggressively, had been accomplished. This plan - full of hope for international cooperation - was to be implemented as soon as the war was over. (Unfortunately, in the Charter for the United Nations, there were just too many veto powers given to too many countries for it ever to be able to it work effectively.)

<u>April 14, 1945</u> – *marched about 22 kms. Lockenny & I are still pretty sick. The R. A. F. really hit nearby last night. Their bombs rocked our barn.*

Meanwhile as the prisoners – along with their weary guards marched - to the west, Allied forces were streaming toward them. On that day, the United States Army split the Ruhr Pocket in two at Hagen. Glider troops captured the ex-German Chancellor von Papen at a hunting lodge near Stockhausen, along with three generals. The French launched a final assault on the trapped German garrison at Bordeaux. The British Second Army reached the outskirts of Bremen, while the U. S. Third Army captured Gera and Bayreuth. The Canadian First Army assumed military control of the Netherlands. In a sort of poetic justice, the German forces there were trapped in the Atlantic wall fortifications they had built along the coastline. What they had so confidently designed as an impregnable defense became an inescapable prison.

Even so, The Black March continued on needlessly – hunger and death keeping step with the men on a daily basis. If they really were ahead of the Russians, why not just point the prisoners toward the Allied lines and let them go? That would certainly have pleased many of the German guards, who also were weary and wanted to go home. Ah! But don't forget the sickened mindset of Bombach and his chief co-conspirators – Pickhardt and Fahnert. Still to this day, no one has been able to figure out how the Nazis had so self-deluded themselves that they couldn't accept the fact that their plan of world domination was unraveling rapidly – right before their eyes.

<u>April 15, 1945</u> - *Sunday – Marched about 24 kms & Lock carried my blankets. He is feeling pretty good but I can hardly eat. We stayed in a nice barn & the old man gave us a 1 ½ of spuds per man.*

April 16, 1945 - *Monday* – *Up bright and early but I feel even worse. We got German rations that consisted of 6 boxes of field crackers and ½ can of liverwurst. As we got these, a P-38 and a BP 47 strafed a train nearby and scared a few of the fellows. A M. E. 110 came over at tree top level. We saw P-47s at their job all day. We marched approx 16 kms and stopped in Annaburg. We are putting up in a day factory with a few airplane parts added. The rumor is that we are cut off and the Yanks are approx 15 miles away. Boy would I like to see those tanks.*

April 18, 1945 – *Wednesday* – *Roll call at 8:00 around 11:30 the P-47s scared the fellows a little because they were strafing too close (500 yds). We rec. a full Red Cross parcel. I traded 3 pks of butts for a lb of coffee. Dewitt got 3 bowls and 3 cups.*

April 19, 1945 – *This morning Dewitt got up and went out & boiled the coffee & I made sandwiches. We got potatoes from the Germans, but the bread hasn't come in yet. Dewitt & I made a birthday cake for him & his wife. Hers is the 20th & his the 21st. We had an early birthday because we ate the cake around 6:00 and had some swell coffee. It is sure nice to eat out of the bowls & drink out of the cups; it seems to taste better than drinking and eating out of cans. They seem to think the war will soon be over.*

There is no indication of how Dewitt got bowls and cups, but it certainly made a difference in attitude. Drinking and eating from a can had been a demeaning experience. Unfortunately the utensils did not get much use because provisions from the Germans trickled down to practically nothing.

April 20, 1945 – *Happy Birthday* – *Mrs. Dewitt & Mr. "Hitler". Good coffee for breakfast. I worked all day helping to set up boilers to cook in. Around 1600 – 1900 B-26s hit an oil dump close by. The windows flew out of the windows and a few of the fellows were really digging in.*

April 21, 1945 – *Sat.* – *Today is Dewitt's birthday (22nd) Gunfire is all around the place. The Russians are too close – so we are moving out. It rained all day and we got good and wet & then slept out in the open (Dalenburg). We crossed the Elbe river on a pontoon bridge.*

<u>April 22, 1945</u> – *Sunday. I got up and built a fire & Lock & I made a stew. After we ate it we made another one. We left the woods and went to small barns. Dewitt went out and stabbed some spuds and we sold them to some of the other fellows (cig. prunes, pate, meat & beans). We made about six stews during the day & Lockeny got a little sick.*

<u>April 23</u> – <u>Monday</u> – *Dewitt & I got the breakfast ready – consisting of toast, Spam, friend potatoes & coffee with milk and sugar added. Pete, Frick & I went into town in search of food. We brought back eggs, jam & bread. Dewitt went into another town & brought back bread, cracker bread, & cheese. Lock had a stew ready & we really had a meal.*

<u>April 24, 1945</u> - *For breakfast toast, eggs, Spam & Coffee. Frick, Pete and I started to town again but a guard caught us and turned us back. Dewitt & Pete went out there & brought back wine, bread, cigars and grain, which we ground to make cereal with. After the stew that Lock made we were notified we had to leave again – Russians too close. Eight of us took off by ourselves & stopped in the town of "Cassa" we made us a bed behind a barn and then had a stew, friend eggs & toast & plenty of coffee.*

Sergeant Lindsay and the other prisoners grew bold as the German guards became increasingly restless and fearful. Everyone knew that the Allied forces were closing in from the West and the Russians from the East – and no one wanted to deal with the Soviets. Jim and his buddies – Dewitt and Lockenny – decided it was time to make a break for freedom. Grabbing an axe from a woodpile they broke into a barn that served as headquarters for the remnants of Stalag Luft IV. The only German inside was a captain. He was only about 5' 6" – one of those 16-year-old kids drafted into the army – and perhaps because of family connections was given his rank. It was obvious that he was scared – actually shaking. Sergeant Lindsay grabbed him by the arms, lifted him up and set him on the edge of a table in the middle of the room. The men stripped the "captain" of his boots and jacket and officer's cap; all the while Lockenny wielded the hatchet in a threatening manner. The captain wet his pants.

The three airmen left him sitting there, laughing as they went. For their mini-escape they had decided to go to the home of a German lady that they had traded with earlier. They intended to spend the night in her barn and get a fresh start the next day. On the way to her home they encountered a gruesome sight. A bloody, headless body, wearing a German uniform, was lying in the ditch alongside of the road. "That looks like Big Stoop," Lockenny declared as he went over to take a closer look.

"How can you tell without his big ugly head?" Dewitt asked. "And in the dark?"

"Just look at the massive size of the body and the corporal's uniform," Lockenny insisted. "It has to be him – I hope it's him. That'd be small revenge for all of our guys he murdered along the way."

April 25, 1945 Wednesday – *For breakfast, coffee, wheat cereal with milk, sugar & prunes, eggs, toast, flapjacks with Jerry Jam after this we all shaved and washed up. The family is very nice & the lady speaks English. She fried the flapjacks. After this we fried potatoes with Spam. Then we mixed another cereal. (Boy we are really eating now.) Before bed we had toasted cheese sandwiches – cake & wine. The stomach is really full.*

April 26 – 1945 – Thursday *This is a day I don't care to forget. About 0400 several people woke us up and tried to get us to leave with them – they were afraid of the Russians. We didn't get up until about six though. We ate 3 eggs, 2 flapjacks, a can of cereal with fresh milk and plenty of coffee. The front lines were supposed to be 11 kms away at Duben. We started out and about 12:30 we came across an outpost. Our soldiers really looked good. They took our names, gave the fellows cigarettes & then took us across the river & fed us – they brought out bread, jam, cereal, milk & coffee. Then they put us on trucks and moved us to Holle. Now we wait our plane.*

The End

At that point he was pleased to stop his account, satisfied that he had faithfully recorded one man's opinion of what it was like to suffer under the Germans.

As Sergeant James B. Lindsay and his companions approached the American fortifications that bright morning, the first reaction of the defenders was one of alarm. The rag tail prisoners coming toward them had no form of insignia, no documentation, and wore a mix of British and American clothing. But, seeing that they were not much more than skin and bones, the GIs welcomed them and began the process that would take them home.

For the *Kriegies* Lindsay had left behind – and were still part of The March - their sleep on the night of April 30th was disturbed with the sounds of Allied guns hitting nearby targets. The drone of planes overhead was incessant. None of the prisoners realized that under the cover of darkness the German guards – including the Commandant and his henchmen - had deserted their posts and slipped away to the west as fast as their feet could carry them. Then at dawn the next day, the prisoners were rocked from their slumber by a sudden, terrific roar, which brought every man to his feet and out into the road to investigate. The sight that greeted them brought their hearts to their throats. The road was aswarm with soldiers from a Canadian tank and paratroops division that had broken through the German lines. Instantly the Canadians were swamped by hoards of hysterically screaming *Kriegies*. The triumphant troops were happily throwing boxes of rations to the ragged men gathered around them. Most of the tossed boxes went unnoticed by the men who were too entranced with the glorious vision of their liberators. They gazed reverently at the Canadians through eyes blinded with tears of gratitude and joy. Nor could they speak over the huge lumps lodged in their throats, but there was no doubt that they were really among friends and finally free. Men alternately cried and laughed as they unashamedly hugged each other. A prayer of thanksgiving welled up in every heart and many fell to their knees to beg forgiveness for having doubted God - for what greater proof of His presence and mercy was there than that glorious day.

After the Canadians had passed, the men had yet to reach Lunenburg, where, in the hands of the British, their liberation became official. Even on this short hike, from Zarratin – their liberation point – to Lunenburg, they were hounded by the fear of recapture since they were marching in a "no man's land". Upon arrival at Lunenburg, trucks transported them to freedom.

The Black March had been a desperate struggle from beginning to end, but it was most bitter in the final weeks when food was scarce and bodies were weak. In those three agonizing months the men had plodded nearly six hundred miles – a remarkable feat considering the weakened physical condition of the men and the grueling circumstances of The March. It had been a tour of Northern Germany on foot – often in blizzard conditions – always without adequate provisions of food and clothing. What a price these stalwart airmen paid in human lives and suffering. Yet they stood tall and loyal to one another and their nation.

Though ignored by most historians, the remainder of those gallant eight thousand American and British Airmen, who stood steady as a unit, are the true and lasting heroes of the triumph over Nazi imperialism.

Epilogue

For Sergeant James B. Lindsay, World War Two effectively ended on April 26, 1945. That is when, of his own accord, he walked a final two miles away from the Germans and into the welcoming arms of the United States Army. He was still able to hold his head high. In the face of horrendous evil and persecution he had never surrendered his dignity. He was one of the 8000 of his comrades who endured and survived the meandering and seemingly meaningless 600 miles of The Black March. (According to his diary, in which he kept a tally of miles marched, he walked 551 miles – the other few miles was by train or ferry. The longest marching day was 40 miles on February 14.) Through snow and ice and rain and skin-numbing wind –17 degrees and 15 inches of snow at one point – churlish guards prodded them forward. Though there were frequent assurances of food coming, more often than not those were but empty promises, and the prisoners had to do without. Along the way hundreds died – murdered by being clubbed by rifle butts, jabbed by bayonets, or a bullet to the head. Starvation and disease and fatigue had been too much for some who slumped at the side of the road – never to be seen again. Though the Germans conducted roll calls along the way, in the aftermath of the war many documents were purposely destroyed so it is impossible to know how many perished in those seemingly endless 87 days. Some estimate that as many as 1300 prisoners died along the way. From reading his diary and understanding the privations that the prisoners suffered, it is a wonder that so many were able to survive. Liberation for the rest of the men came at dawn on May 1, when units of the Canadian Army swarmed through the German lines. The next day the prisoners continued westward on their own until they reached Luneburg, where, in the hands of the British, their freedom became official.

For Adolph Hitler the war had ended a day earlier – April 30, 1945. Months before that, on January 16, 1945, he had taken up residency at the *Fuhrerbunker* in Berlin - and like a rat, he never again left his cellar dwelling. From there, cut off from the view of the world, the once proud and exceedingly boastful dictator presided over what had become a rapid disintegration of the Third Reich. This evil creation by Hitler and his henchmen was supposed to have lasted for a thousand years. Now, after just twelve years of power (Hitler had been named Chancellor of Germany on January 30, 1933), the Allied Forces were advancing speedily against the Germans from the east and the west. By late April, Soviet soldiers entered the capitol city and were moving steadily toward the center where the Chancellery – the site of power and authority - was located. After midnight on April 29th, Hitler surrendered to his mistress Eva Braun and married her in a civil ceremony. They then lived as husband and wife in the bunker for about forty hours before entering a suicide pact at 3:30 in the afternoon on the 30th. Life ended for the two of them ignominiously – she by cyanide poison and he by a pistol shot to the head.

For everyone else the War in Europe ended a week later - May 5, 1945. General Alfred Jodl, the German Chief of Staff, signed the unconditional surrender of Germany to the Western Allies and Russia. All operations were to cease at one minute after midnight on the 8th of May.

For many the nightmare was finally over! Or was it? Could the world ever recover from such a murderous ordeal? By wanton brutality an estimated 60 million people – six million just because they were Jewish - died because of the menace of the Nazi mentality of evil.

He did not live to see the aftermath, but before his death, Franklin Roosevelt had begun to realize dreadful handwriting on the wall as a result of some of his major mistakes of judgment - because of commitments he had made to the Soviets. He had been in a close league of cooperation with Joseph Stalin against the German peril, assuming that the threat of communism from such a backward country was not nearly so great as that from the militaristic Nazis. In fact, through Roosevelt the "Lend Lease" (so called) program provided millions of tons of armaments and foodstuffs to the Soviets. (None of which the Russians ever repaid.) As seen earlier, Roosevelt and Churchill had made secret deals with Stalin at their Yalta Conference; but Roosevelt saw too late how foolish it had been, and that Stalin couldn't be trusted. During March of 1945, President Roosevelt sent several messages to the Soviet dictator accusing him of breaking agreements he had made on Poland, Germany, Prisoners of War, and other issues. Stalin's stolid response was to accuse the Allies of trying to broker a separate peace with Hitler behind his back. (Indeed the Americans did conduct secret talks with the Germans. Allan Dulles, who was later to head the CIA, met with members of the German High Command - General von Vietinghoff and SS General Wolff - on March 13,1945 in Bern, Switzerland to arrange for the early surrender of German forces in northern Italy.)

As it turned out, the extreme fear that the Germans had of being captured by the Russians might well have saved Jim Lindsay and other prisoners from being swallowed up in the Soviet Archipelago – never to be heard of again. The appalling Black March toward the west was devised to avoid such a disaster. Though the prisoners suffered terribly without sanitation or sustaining food and water, the March did result in their escape from the greater unthinkable horrors of being taken by the Red Army.

Thankfully, for Sergeant Lindsay that didn't happen. Within hours of crossing into U.S. held territory, his processing began. Because thousands of Germans were deserting their posts, and fleeing to the west, it became a painstaking procedure for allied authorities to check the credentials of every man. Of course Lindsay had no proof of his identity, so it took days to locate his military records and confirm his story. Meanwhile he was at least able to have a shower, change into clean clothes, and throw away the rags of his imprisonment. Once he had good food on a consistent basis, he began to realize how tired he was. He and the other brave men of The Black March had trudged forward on mere grit and will power – never with any semblance of lodging and consequently short of good sleep. Without proper food and rest their bodies had become almost skeletal - hollow eyes stared out from sunken cheeks - stomachs curved inward. On his second day in freedom, having eaten well and with a comfortable bed at his disposal, he slept around the clock and more – sixteen hours straight.

He was eager to get in contact with his family, to tell them he was alive and well. The Army, of course overwhelmed with the sudden turn of events, asked him to be patient. He wrote a letter to his mother right away, but before it arrived she received a Western Union Telegram – she and her husband were ecstatic. Though the message was brief it was far more encouraging than the ones they had grieved over at the first of the year:

May 11, 1945, T/Sgt Hames B. Lindsay, 15081658, requests Mrs. Ben Lindsay, 414 South Main be notified his liberation.

That was followed by a second telegram on May 23 from the Adjutant General:

The Secretary of War desires me to inform you that your son T/Sgt Lindsay, James B. returned to military control.

Two weeks later he arrived home, with time to spare to fulfill his prediction, "I will be eating strawberry shortcake for my birthday on June 16 in Kokomo, Indiana." Outwardly he didn't look any the worse for the wear, having gained back all but five pounds of the weight lost during his incarceration. Inwardly, however, he had become a much more mature man. At only twenty-one years of age he had experienced both the extreme ugliness of the inhumanity of man-to-man by the Germans, and the beauty of the comradeship with his fellow prisoners. He spoke glowingly of the latter, even to the point of tears. He would never forget those who carried his pack when he was so weak he could hardly walk - and who shared a bit of a chocolate bar when that is all they had. On the other hand, he chose largely to ignore mention of his captors. He did not forgive, but he did choose to begin to forget. Amazingly, his family seemed to understand, and didn't ply him with endless questions.

"I kept a diary all the time I was in Germany," he told them. "You're welcome to read it. But it isn't pretty." His youngest brother just looked at him in awe - content just to sit very, very close to his hero on the maroon couch in the living room.

Although he had not yet renewed all of his strength, Jim was restless to make an agonizing trip across four states to visit face-to-face with the families of his fellow B-17 crewmembers. Though the war was over, those fathers and mothers had no closure until the lone survivor arrived to confirm their worst fears. It was not a pleasant task, but one he knew he had to do. It was gut wrenching for him to see the anguish in their faces and tears in their eyes, but it gave him an even greater appreciation for his own miraculous survival.

The Army Air Force had given him a sixty-day furlough. When a reporter from the Kokomo Tribune asked, "Have you experienced enough of war?" He answered, "Yes and no. I hope to be sent to the Pacific area to do my part in cleaning up the mess there."

But that was not to be. The War in the Pacific ended with the unconditional surrender of Japan on August 16 – after two horrific atomic bombs had obliterated Hiroshima and Nagasaki. Two weeks later on September 2, 1945, in memorable fashion, on the Battleship Missouri in Tokyo Bay, the generals and admirals of the Imperial Forces of Japan signed the papers of unconditional surrender.

With the war concluded, there were strong demands for prosecution of those responsible for crimes against humanity – under the guise of war.

When the main body of the remnants of Stalag IV came under British control, rudimentary interviews of the prisoners were made, and the process began to determine if war crimes had been committed. Sergeant Frank Paules' testimony recorded in chapter seven was typical of the information prosecutors obtained. But soon the charges against members of the German government and military became overwhelming. In the months following the conclusion of hostilities, more than 8,000 cases were examined, naming 37,000 German officers and guards as having purposely committed criminal acts against defenseless prisoners. (This, of course, was miniscule in comparison to the burgeoning stories of atrocities from the hundreds of concentration and extermination camps devised by the Jew-hating Nazis.)

The four-day journey/transfer of 2000 prisoners from Stalag VI to Stalag IV in mid-July 1944 became a center of focus for prosecutors. In his deposition Paules made three detailed charges:

1. *On board the ship ...prisoners were crowded into the hold ... without provisions for hygienic necessities ... or water ... no life preservers were provided ... conditions were enforced for over 40 hours.*

2. *Upon disembarking, prisoners were handcuffed for the duration of their journey ... then forced to march from the train ... in the charge of guards with fixed bayonets and dogs ... making it impossible to carry their baggage.*
3. *Upon arrival at KGF lager nr.4 ... the prisoners ... were struck with gun butts and subjected to insults ... others suffered bayonet wounds. I protest that these points were violations of the Geneva Convention relative to prisoners of war ... to be observed by the German Military Authorities.*

Taking these and other testimonies under consideration, on October 5, Albert Kadler, a Swiss delegate to the United Nations War Crimes Commission made an exhaustively complete account of the four-day journey from Hydekrug to Kiefeheide. This document became the early basis for the British and American prosecutors' claims that a war crime had occurred. In his report Kadler had included an opinion that camp administrators, rather than their superiors, could be held responsible.

For their part, the British pursued an aggressive policy of punishment for war crimes. By May of 1946 the United Kingdom had filed 1077 cases, compared to only 318 by the United States. Of these, there were a total of nine cases against the Commandant, officers and guards of Stalag Luft IV.

The legal machinery for the investigation, apprehension, and trials of the war criminals actually had begun in January 1944, while the war was still in progress. Aware of the brutal behavior against prisoners by the Germans – and even more so by the Japanese - the Judge Advocate was directed to establish a War Crimes Office. Later, a coalition was put together of representatives from the Navy, the War Department, and State Department to oversee these matters, which led to establishing War Crimes offices in both the Pacific and European theaters.

It was a difficult task to identify and track down thousands of suspects across Europe. The actual filing of a War Crimes Brief on October 6, 1945, indicting personnel of Stalag IV was (for that moment) a watershed event. As evidence accumulated, the case was named for Walther Pickhardt, who was considered to be the major perpetrator. At least six provisions of the Geneva Convention had been violated, but the main thrust involved Articles 2 and 11, which dealt with the assault and unlawful wounding of prisoners. Article 2 reads in part:

Prisoners are in the power of hostile governments, but not of individuals. They shall at all times be treated humanely, particularly against acts of violence … and measures of reprisal.

Pickhardt, Col. Aribert Bombach, Reinhard Fahnert, and Hans Schmidt were held responsible for an organized reign of terror, lasting from July 1944 until May 1945. During the time of their oversight, at least four unarmed American POWs had been shot in Stalag Luft IV. They also had been in charge of the transfer of the 2000 prisoners from Stalag VI to Stalag IV, which was carried out with extreme and unnecessarily cruel conditions. The most atrocious acts of mistreatment and deaths of prisoners by these men, of course, were during The Black March.

Included in the accumulated evidence were some extraordinary documents detailing the arrest reports for three of the accused: Pickhardt, Bombach, and Fahnert. They had been picked up on November 11, 1945 in Austria just south of Salzburg. At 10 p.m., in the town of Kukels (a stone's throw from Berchtesgarten) Aribert Bombach was apprehended. His arrest warrant stated:

Information was received that this man is wanted as a war criminal by the U. S. A. for ill-treatment of American POWs. A quantity of cigarettes and food from Red Cross parcels was found in possession of a woman living with the accused. This property was believed looted from the camp.

An hour later Reinhard Fahnert was arrested at the same location with the notation:

Former Abwehr N.C.O. of Luft Stalag 4 – suspected war criminal.

The three, formerly proud leaders of the prison camp, were photographed and numbered for the criminal record:
Bombach, Aribert Otto was #29 18382
Fahnert, Reinhard was # 29 18383
Pickhardt, Walther was #29 16873

Prosecutors tried to piece together a case file concerning the shooting deaths of Aubry Teague, George Walker, Walter Getsey and Walter Niles. The identity of the guards involved, however, remained a mystery. Liberated prisoners gave testimony to what they experienced, but the camp documents had been buried when Stalag IV was evacuated – and that location was now in Poland – and under Soviet control.

As months wore on, all the cases were consolidated into one under the name of Pickhardt. Lager officers Schliep, Wienart, Zallman and Wolf were added to the growing list of the accused, and the file was ready for prosecution. In its final form, Register #1648 – "United States against Germany – case #1", named 14 officers and guards as perpetrators of crimes against prisoners during the evacuation of Luft 6 and afterwards at Luft 4. Their shadowy world was thrown open to public view, revealing their immoral character and vile deeds for the record.

Nonetheless, in spite of the capture of Pickhardt, Bombach, and Fahnert, the case languished on procedural matters. In 1946, special agents were sent out to confirm the identities of the three who had been caught. They showed photos to a number of those former prisoners who had witnessed the atrocities, and their identities were affirmed. But there were few German records obtained by the Judge Advocate. Consequently, amazingly no "paper link" could be established between the accused and the alleged events. In a letter dated September 19, 1947, Maj. Walter L. Parker wrote the unfortunate epitaph for the case:

This case consists of 58 volumes of testimony, 44 of which are statements of liberated prisoners. No further investigation has been made of this case because of the highly contradictory nature of the statements. A thorough investigation would be necessary to prepare for trial and would be much more difficult than normal because the camp is in Poland. The attitude of local witnesses may have changed with the lapse of time.

A good many leads are offered. Among them are records buried at the camp and pictures from which other perpetrators might be identified – if they could be located.

It does not appear that the case can be developed into a triable murder category. Bomcach, Pickhardt, and Fahnert are the only ones ever to have been in our custody – and they have been released.

So, for the persecuted prisoners of Stalag IV – the bedraggled survivors of the infamous Black March – and their tormentors, the German officers and guards – the war finally ended on September 19, 1947. Then, even though it had the power to do so, the United States government did nothing in this particular case to redeem the honor of its valiant fighting men. Bombach and his underlings were allowed to slither into obscurity – never prosecuted for the evil they had done against helpless prisoners. The only possible retribution ever affected might have been the unsubstantiated death of the headless body, assumed to be "Big Stoop" – which Lindsay and his buddies saw on the night of their escape.

From the viewpoint of "justice" for the victims of unparalleled horror, the Western Allies handled the pursuit of German war criminals poorly. Only a few hundred of the thousands who were involved in atrocious acts against innocent victims were made to pay for their crimes. This could be partly attributed to the fact that from the beginning the American and British standard of jurisprudence – "innocent until proven guilty" – was invoked. (The Russians, on the other hand, didn't worry about conducting trials. As shown previously in chapter two, they simply liquidated nearly every captured German in their control – with no consideration of guilt.) Since the Germans destroyed tons of records as the war was coming to an end, "proof" was often difficult, indeed impossible to find.

Nonetheless, by the fall of 1946 the War Crimes Tribunal was prepared for its case against 22 of the highest-ranking members of the Nazi regime. (Martin Bormann was tried in absentia even though it was widely believed that a Russian soldier had shot him dead when he tried to slip away from Hitler's Command Bunker.) After a lengthy trial in Nuremberg, Germany, 19 of the accused were convicted and 3 were acquitted. Twelve were condemned to death by hanging (including Bormann), seven were given prison sentences ranging from a few years to life, and three committed suicide. Though he was watched closely, Hermann Goering – the highest ranking Nazi convicted – escaped the hangman's noose by succeeding to commit suicide with a cyanide capsule in his cell two hours before he was to be led to the gallows.

In spite of many failures on the part of prosecutors to bring guilty

Germans to justice, there was one tribunal that was precise and that exacted the ultimate penalty for the perpetrators. Interestingly, the circumstances of that case ran quite similar to Jim Lindsay's experience, but with a far more tragic ending.

Bill Dodd, like Lindsay, was also trained as a machine gunner on a B-17 Flying Fortress. Three months before Sergeant Lindsay's adventures began, on August 4, 1944, flying from an airbase in England, Dodd was on his third mission over Germany. Antiaircraft fire hit another plane in the formation, which caused it to clip Dodd's plane and cripple it. The crew didn't panic – even though they knew they would have to abandon the aircraft over enemy territory. In orderly fashion, they bailed out and all landed safely on the small island of Borkum in the North Sea. (Borkum was a strategic military site for Germany. It was from there on August 2, 1934 that the Germans test fired the first two of its A-2 rockets. Development and improvement of the massively destructive weapon continued throughout the war – and wrecked great havoc on England.) The ten airmen from the B-17 were quickly rounded up and captured. But instead of being treated honorably as Prisoners of War, they were marched through the town and down to the sea. Along the way they were beaten by the townspeople, screamed at and pummeled mercilessly. Then when they got to the sea, they were lined up and shot dead. Bill was only 22.

At the time, no one in the U. S. military was aware of what had happened, only that the plane had gone down. That her son was missing in action was all that Mrs. Dodd knew until after the war. By means of a thorough investigation, however, the truth was uncovered. The bodies of Bill Dodd and his crewmates were exhumed and buried with honor at a military cemetery in Belgium. A year later a war crimes trial was conducted. The mayor of Borkum and four German officers were found guilty of the murders and sentenced to hang.

As was the case with thousands of others in the war, Bill Dodd was an unlikely hero. In fact, he didn't even have to be in the war. In 1943 he was a student at the University of Notre Dame in South Bend, Indiana; and since he hadn't been drafted he could have finished out his studies. But that option didn't appeal to him. His country was at war and needed him, and he chose to a part of the fight for freedom.

Men like Jim Lindsay and Bill Dodd were not unique among the men of their day. There were millions of other just like them – and women too - ready to do their duty for God and country. The population of the United States was only 133 million in 1941, when the charm of a rather rural nation was transformed – practically overnight into an industrial powerhouse. In four years of global warfare those men and women rose to the challenge of their day. Not only did ten percent of them fight on the battlefields of the world, the rest worked arduously to feed and arm the rest of the free world. No wonder they are referred to as the Great Generation.

The Lend Lease Act passed by Congress in the spring of 1941 ended any pretense of neutrality on the part of Washington. Hitler harangued on what he called this great duplicity when he declared war on the United States four days after Pearl Harbor – December 11, 1941. This gigantic output on the part of the Americans was a determining factor in the outcome of the war. In four years time the United States sent more than $50 billion in aide to its Allies. (This would be the equivalent of $870 billion in 2010 dollars.) Implicit in this plan was that after the conclusion of hostilities there would be an accounting and the United States would be repaid for any overages. Tiny Finland was the first to repay – before it was swallowed up by the Soviet Union. The Russians never paid a dime – and the United Kingdom finally settled the account 51 years after the war – in 2006.

Yet, what would be the course of history without the unbelievable industrial output from the United States? At last the ambition of Alexander Hamilton (in 1789 the first Treasurer of the United States) was realized as the free enterprise system proved its ability to meet this enormous demand for "stuff". No longer would the "land of the free" be isolated – insolated from the world. With its victorious leadership in overcoming the militaristic designs of the Axis Powers, it was thrust forward as a "Super Power".

In only four years the world of Jim Lindsay was transformed – exploded. Neither he nor anyone else could ever return to the idyllic lifestyle of his youth. But would he still want to go on another hunger strike, in order to be involved? You betcha!

Postlude

While still on furlough in 1945, before his return to action, Jim Lindsay had another significant event in his life. The day after his 21st, birthday he met a beautiful young woman, Virginia Gray, and proposed to her the next day at the historic bridge at Highland Park in Kokomo. They married on their third day together. Such hasty romances are often troubled and short lived, but theirs lasted nearly fifty-four years – until her death on July 1, 1998.

With the war having come to an end, Jim separated from the Air Force, and he and his bride went into business and started a small (twenty-seat), home-cooked-food restaurant on Markland Avenue in Kokomo. It did not go well. In two weeks time they closed up shop and Jim reenlisted in the Air Force. He then served as a Non-commissioned Officer for another quarter-of-a-century, before retiring to a successful business career in Reno, Nevada. He died on February 19, 2001, and was buried with full military honors at the Veterans Memorial Park in Fernley, Nevada. Both of his sons, Sandford Benjamin and James Bryan, followed in his footsteps with careers in the Air Force. He and Virginia also parented two lovely daughters, Deborah and Virginia Lil.

The younger sister summed up the thoughts for the family: "Our father gave each of us his strength to succeed in life, love, and happiness; and gave us a family which we cherish. Just like him we all love strawberry shortcake – and it brings lots of hope.

In 1992, the American survivors of the Black March funded and dedicated a memorial at the former site of Stalag Luft IV in Poland - the starting place of a March that is an important part of United States Air Force history. It recognizes and honors those many heroes for their valor.

Diary Picture Section

Sergeant James B. Lindsay

SERVICE RECORD

NAME *T/Sgt. James B. Lindsay*

ADDRESS *414 South Main Street - Kokomo Indiana*

SERIAL NO. *15081658*   *Army Air Force*

ENTERED SERVICE

DATE *5th September - 1941*

PLACE *Kokomo, Indiana*

BRANCH OF SERVICE *Army Air Force*

REMARKS *Re-enlisted 10th June 1946*

FT. BENJ. HARRISON, IND   September 9, 1941
(Reception or Replacement Center)   (Date)

This is to advise you that

Pvt. James B. Lindsay,   15081658
(Name and Army Serial Number)

has this date been assigned to _____
(Organization, Replacement Center, or other installation)

His post office address is: _____ Jefferson Barracks, Missouri

This card to be filled out for each man at Reception or Replacement Center, upon
assignment. He will be required to address the card and mail it to his nearest
relative.

W. D., A. G. O. Form No. 203
February 15, 1941

16—21276 · U. S. GOVERNMENT PRINTING OFFICE

UNITED STATES ARMY RECRUITING SERVICE

Fort Benjamin Harrison, Ind.
....
Place

Sept. 5th, 1941
....
Date

This letter is to advise you that .... James Benjamin Lindsay ....

enlisted on .... Sept. 5th, 1941 .... in the Regular Army of the United States for

Air Corps, JeffersonBks., Missouri ......, for a period of .. three (3) .... years.
(Branch)   (Station)

He gave his age as .. 18 .... years .... 2 . months, and stated that he ~~has~~ is not

married, and that no one is dependent upon him for support. He named as his nearest relative

..... Verda M. Lindsay .... (Mother) .... 700 North Bell St., Kokomo, Indiana ....
(Name)   (Relationship)   (Address)

and .... Same as above ....
(Name)   (Relationship)   (Address)

as the person to be notified in case of emergency.

The form for written consent to his enlistment in the Regular Army bears the signature of

.... None .... None .... None ....
(Name)   (Relationship)   (Address)

Should any of the statements made by the soldier, as indicated above, be incorrect or misleading, or if there is any other irregularity in connection with his application for enlistment of which you are aware, it would be proper for you to communicate this knowledge to his Commanding Officer. For this purpose there is enclosed an official envelope, which requires no postage, addressed to his first Commanding Officer.

This letter has been shown to the soldier in order that he may reaffirm the answers he gave, as indicated above, to questions in connection with his application for enlistment.

* **Strike out words that do not apply.**

....
Signature of Recruiting Officer

J. G. KIPLINGER, 1st Lt. Inf.
....
Rank

F-12—RPB

RPB—10-22-40—100M

113

WESTERN UNION

A. N. WILLIAMS
PRESIDENT

1201

The filing time shown in the date line on telegrams and day letters is STANDARD TIME at point of origin. Time of receipt is STANDARD TIME at point of destination

C47 43 GOVT=WUX WASHINGTON DC 26 426P

MRS VERDA M LINDSAY=

414 SOUTH MAIN ST

1944 NOV 26 PM 4 23

THE SECRETARY OF WAR DESIRES ME TO EXPRESS HIS DEEP REGRET THAT YOUR SON TECHNICAL SERGEANT JAMES B LINDSAY HAS BEEN REPORTED MISSING IN ACTION SINCE ELEVEN NOV OVER ITALY IF FURTHER DETAILS OR OTHER INFORMATION ARE RECEIVED YOU WILL BE PROMPTLY NOTIFIED=

WITSELL ACTING THE ADJUTANT GENERAL=

THE COMPANY WILL APPRECIATE SUGGESTIONS FROM ITS PATRONS CONCERNING ITS SERVICE

WESTERN UNION

A. N. WILLIAMS
PRESIDENT

1201

The filing time shown in the date line on telegrams and day letters is STANDARD TIME at point of origin. Time of receipt is STANDARD TIME at point of destination

1944 DEC 31 PM 4 51

C30 34 GOVT=WUX WASHINGTON DC 31 442P

MRS VERDA M LINDSAY=

414 SOUTH MAIN ST

REPORT JUST RECEIVED THROUGH THE INTERNATIONAL RED CROSS STATES THAT YOUR SON TECHNICAL SERGEANT JAMES B LINDSAY IS A PRIOSONER OF WAR OF THE GERMAN GOVERNMENT LETTER OF INFORMATION FOLLOWS FROM PROVOST MARSHAL GENERAL=

DUNLOP ACTING THE ADJUTANT GENERAL=

gmp

WAR DEPARTMENT
THE ADJUTANT GENERAL'S OFFICE
WASHINGTON 25, D. C.

IN REPLY REFER TO:

AG 201 Lindsay, James B.
PC-N MTO 301

28 November 1944

Mrs. Verda M. Lindsay
414 South Main Street
Kokomo, Indiana

Dear Mrs. Lindsay:

This letter is to confirm my recent telegram in which you were
regretfully informed that your son, Technical Sergeant James B. Lindsay,
15,081,658, Air Corps, has been reported missing in action since 11 November
1944 over Italy.

I know that added distress is caused by failure to receive more
information or details. Therefore, I wish to assure you that at any time
additional information is received it will be transmitted to you without
delay, and, if in the meantime no additional information is received, I
will again communicate with you at the expiration of three months. Also,
it is the policy of the Commanding General of the Army Air Forces upon receipt of the "Missing Air Crew Report" to convey to you any details that
might be contained in that report.

The term "missing in action" is used only to indicate that the
whereabouts or status of an individual is not immediately known. It is
not intended to convey the impression that the case is closed. I wish to
emphasize that every effort is exerted continuously to clear up the status
of our personnel. Under war conditions this is a difficult task as you
must readily realize. Experience has shown that many persons reported
missing in action are subsequently reported as prisoners of war, but as
this information is furnished by countries with which we are at war, the
War Department is helpless to expedite such reports.

The personal effects of an individual missing overseas are held
by his unit for a period of time and are then sent to the Effects Quartermaster, Kansas City, Missouri, for disposition as designated by the soldier.

Permit me to extend to you my heartfelt sympathy during this
period of uncertainty.

Sincerely yours,

J. A. ULIO
Major General,
The Adjutant General.

1 Inclosure
    Bulletin of Information.

115

STALAG LUFT IV

Photo looking into Stalag Luft IV. (http://www.b24.net/)

"A" Lager - the backs of Barracks #1, 2 & 3, taken from a guard tower.

Stalag Luft IV: Lager (Compound) A Barracks 1,2 &3.

Appell circa 6/44

LUFT4

Burial Aubrey Teague
6/44 Luft 4

Ball game lagar A

Marching into
Vorlagar

Feb 6 '45 evacuation
Luft 4

OFFICERS IN CHARGE OF LUFT IV

Col Aribert Bombach

Hauptman Richard Pickhardt

Captain Reinhard Fahnert

ROUTE OF THE BLACK MARCH

Map of Germany showing the route of the infamous "BLACK MARCH".

The filing time shown in the date line on telegrams and day letters is STANDARD TIME at point of origin. Time of receipt is STANDARD TIME at point of destination

C 94 20/19=WUX WASHINGTON DC 13 338P   1945 MAY 13 PM 4 24

HOME SERVICE ARC=
2001/2 NORTH BUCKEYE ST

MAY 11 1945 T/SGT HAMES B LINDSAY 15081658 REQUESTS MRS
BEN LINDSAY 414 SOUTH MAIN BE NOTIFIED HIS LIBERATION=
MARGARET SHOTTON NATL HS.

11 1945 15081658 414

filing time shown in the date line on telegrams and day letters is STANDARD TIME at point of origin. Time of receipt is STANDARD TIME at point of destination

C201 20 GOVT=WUX WASHINGTON DC 23 429P
MRS VERDA M LINDSAY=   1945 MAY 23 PM 4 30
414 S MAIN KOKOMO IND=

THE SECRETARY OF WAR DESIRES ME TO INFORM YOU THAT YOUR
SON T/SGT LINDSAY JAMES B RETURNED TO MILITARY CONTROL=
JA ULIO THE ADJUTANT GENERAL.

T/SGT

119

Stalag Luft IV Monument dedicated on September 4, 1992

The unveiling of the Luft IV Memorial, at the center of what remains of the Camp site, was the culmination of true international cooperation. The first attempts to recognize the importance of the site began ten years earlier, with a sign placed at a nearby crossroads. In 1988, a large stone with a bronze plaque was placed near the center of what remained of the camp.

PRISONER OF W◼◼◼◼ST
KRIEGSGEFANGENENPOST
SERVICE DES PRISONNIERS DE GUERRE

BY AIR MAIL
PAR AVION

AFFIX
6¢
POSTAGE

RANK AND NAME *The way Gans got letters* ....
(CAPITAL LETTERS) UNITED STATES PRISONER OF WAR.

PRISONER OF WAR No. ....
(SEE NOTE ON FLAP)

CAMP NAME AND No. *While a German*

SUBSIDIARY CAMP No. *Prisoner*

COUNTRY ....

VIA NEW YORK, N. Y.

IMPORTANT: FOR PRISONERS IN GERMAN HANDS THE PRISONER OF WAR NUMBER SHOULD BE CLEARLY INDICATED IF KNOWN. IT MUST NOT BE CONFUSED WITH THE ARMY SERIAL NUMBER.

About the Author

Arthur L. Lindsay is active as a public speaker, having spoken in ten countries on four continents. He is the father of four Tedrin, Timothy, Linda, and Colin.

Art has been a resident of Lincoln, Nebraska since 1988. Though he has many interests, his primary focus is on his own personal relationship with Jesus Christ. Therefore, he steadily studies and memorizes the Word of God. Second to that, he loves to share his faith with men in one-on-one discipleship training. Additionally he has been involved in prison ministry for more than fifty years.

He is the author of eleven previous books. Four of them are biographies: *I Can: Coach Ron Brown's Search for Success; Not Even a Thread: When a rapist repents ...God; One Final Pass: the Brook Berringer story;* and *I Can 2.* There have been four previous histories written by request: *It Takes a Home: Commemorating 90 years of service of People's City Mission; Most Unusual Packages, the story of Bethphage; Influence, a history of the Nebraska Fellowship of Christian Athletes;* and *A Tree Grows in Lincoln, a history of Christ Temple Church.* Art has also written a novel, *Three Wings Against the Monkey;* and two books on ethics for the insurance industry: *Don't Punt* and *Cover All the Bases.*